To Dan & Amanda Ritter
Love & peace!
Emery R. Tang
05m

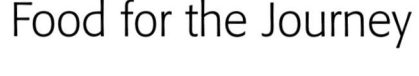
Food for the Journey

by
Emery R. Tang

2004
Castle Press
Pasadena, California

Copyright © 2004 by Emery R. Tang

ISBN 0-9669263-0-7

Layout Design – Fernando Muñoz

Photography – Emery R. Tang

Published by Franciscan Friars
20444 Magnolia Street
Huntington Beach, CA 92646-5212

E-mail: etofm@socal.rr.com

Life is a journey through lights and shadows toward a greater life.

To all who prompted and prodded and pushed...

Contents

1	Open Parentheses	1
2	Chisel on Marble	7
3	How to Love Myself	11
4	The Light of Truth	15
5	Billions of Blind Mice	19
6	La Suegra y Nuera (Mother-and Daughter-in-law)	23
7	The Real Miracles	27
8	There Oughtta Be a Law	31
9	God Rested. God *Rested?!*	35
10	The Beautiful Leper	39
11	My Treasure	43
12	Success	47
13	The Beast With Seven Heads	51
14	The Secret That Shouldn't Be	57
15	Let Me Do It For You	61
16	Beware The Gift With a Hook	65
17	Saying It With Flowers	69

18	The Big Difference	73
19	Covenant	77
20	New Cloth & A New Wineskin	83
21	And Now for the Truth...Until Now it has Been B.C.–From Now on it is A.D.	87
22	Passing The Jewel	93
23	A Kingdom of Kids	97
24	The Gift of Blindness	101
25	About Birds, Bees and Humans	105
26	Recycling Paper, Bottles & Souls	111
27	Forgiveness, The Highest Love	115
28	When Weak is Strong	119
29	Must Joy Always Bring Twin Sister, Pain, Along?	123
30	In Deepest Gratitude	127
31	My Church	131
32	Keeping The Appointment	135
33	Close Parentheses	139

Foreword

Anyone who knows E. T., Emery Tang, knows the least "alien" human being on planet earth. Humor, humility, humaneness – E. T. has it all.

And it's captured in his extraordinary tour de force: FOOD FOR THE JOURNEY.

Realistic spirituality flows from an integrated personality equally at home with awesome Divinity or flawsome humanity. This rare volume liberates not only the beauty of a gifted soul, but displays the touching talent of perceptive eyes that collect the beauty that surrounds us…E. T.'s photos are breathtaking.

For Fr. Emery, God is mankind's most relentless champion who will settle for nothing less until the worst of us are safe and sound in His presence. Unconditional love is another way of saying Eternal Life!

These pages are a treat for anyone with a taste for living and loving; a tonic for the lost and the lonely. FOOD FOR THE JOURNEY – a spiritual vitamin pack!

Whatever the nutrient in one's credal diet, be it meaty or meager, FOOD FOR THE JOURNEY is healthy fare for the hungry heart. It is a savory serving with seasoned TANG at his zesty best.

Bon appetit!

Monsignor Joseph M. Wadowicz
Author: *The Now Testament*

You never walk alone.

food for the journey
by
Emery R. Tang

A collection of reflective essays and photos containing personal discoveries and insights that may nourish other travelers on their spiritual journey.

The mystery of life is like a dense cloud covering the universe. Occasionally there comes a shaft of marvelous light and understanding that breaks through to offer spectacular glimpses into the "Unfathomable Riches" beyond.

When Jesus dispatched his disciples to preach the Gospel to every creature (Mk. 16:6), he meant that his Good News was to be shared, understood and lived by every man, woman and child. It was not to be a private gold mine of beauty and truth accessible only to an intellectual elite or privileged sect.

The most challenging aspect of this task has been to present the sublime, profound truths of the Gospel in as direct and uncomplicated way as possible. "Let your words be simple," St. Francis urged his preaching brothers.

Just as Jesus used homely, picturesque analogies and stories to describe his wonderful kingdom--a work in progress--, so I have included photographic images - picture parables--, to add a further dimension to the truth under consideration.

Finally, I have sprinkled amusing stories throughout that are meant to lend emphasis in a non-threatening way. I am personally convinced that Jesus used humor in his engaging manner of presentation and story telling. A good story, after all, deserves to be preserved and shared, making a lesson palatable and bringing joy simultaneously.

-ET

*Blessed with faith, family and friends.
What will this boy become?*

Open Parentheses

"Before the world was made, God chose us to live in his presence through love."
(Eph. 1:4)

    I've been told - and I accept on faith - that I was born in 1927. Even though I wasn't aware of it happening to me and certainly had no choice in the matter, I've been here on the earth ever since, reflecting on the what, where, when, how and why of my life. My parents who are responsible for my being alive have lived their lives and gone on. It's impossible for me to overstate my appreciation and gratitude to them for all the pain and suffering they endured—and the faith they practiced—when all ten pounds of me arrived, and I began to grow and develop under their loving care.

    Since birth is the beginning of a life that is filled with virtually unlimited possibilities and surprises, I compare it to the opening of parentheses. When my life ends, the parentheses will close. And while I've had schoolmates whose parentheses closed tragically as early as ten years of age, my own life has already lasted seven times as long. Life has been a most precious gift, narrowly escaping closure a few times through illness, auto accidents and near drowning.

    My earliest memory dates to 1933. I was standing on a curb in south Phoenix, which means that I was only six years old. How do I know that? Because for some strange reason I clearly remember reading a copper license plate on a parked car that read "1933." In those early days Arizona was a newborn state and played loose with her native wealth as The Copper State by issuing copper license plates.

At the time I had entered second grade in St. Mary's school and was also attending Chinese school and had learned how to write my name and to read simple lessons in Chinese. By age six I was hungrily learning to read English and spell everything in sight. Pronunciation however was another matter.

One of my most embarrassing moments was when Sister picked me to recite a patriotic poem from our reader. "Read it with feeling," she urged. Proudly clearing my throat, I began melodramatically: "Hats off, the flag is passing by! A blare of bugles…" which I pronounced "buggles." Gales of laughter rocked the room. I melted into my seat in tears of shame.

I was number four of nine surviving siblings, each born at home. I have faint memories of a midwife in the house, pails of bloody water in the bathroom, and the familiar cries of a newborn baby coming from mother's bedroom. Yet I never knew where babies came from. Each of us arrived with regularity, about a year and a half apart, boy followed by girl. Naturally we concluded that male and female babies always took turns arriving.

As I've become more aware of the times we lived in, it has dawned on me that, although we were all born at the height (depth?) of the Great Depression, we never seemed to want for anything. This is a tribute to the courage, resourcefulness and faith of my parents, particularly my father. He had immigrated to America about fifteen years before the Depression and yet had managed to establish a successful wholesale grocery business in that tumultuous period, when so many people suffered financial ruin.

When I recall other details of my early childhood, it's a wonder that my parents didn't become discouraged and decide to stop having children after me. To begin with, they were wracked with worry when pernicious pneumonia nearly snuffed out my infant life in the first year. On the other hand, they may have entertained fleeting thoughts of disowning me a few years later.

One fateful day I was playing with matches. As it happened, I accidentally set fire to Aunt Mary's house next door. I can still hear the screaming fire engines racing to the house, smell the acrid smoke and see the scorched, wet paneling on the side of her house.

I continued to add fuel to the fire. At family gatherings today my sisters persist in retelling about the time when several of them were taking their Saturday bath. Hearing their splashing and giggling, I propped a ladder against the wall to have a look. Their screams of alarm alerted my mother who came after me with a switch torn from a tamarack tree.

But there was more to come. My bewildered parents surely must have thought me "bad seed" when Uncle Charley, mother's brother, called one day from his corner grocery store. He reported that he was missing a shiny, red pocketknife from his display case, and that I was the likely culprit.

Well, I was. Humiliated, mother administered swift justice to my backside, sent me back to return the hot goods and to 'fess up to Uncle Charley, who was not well known for his geniality. The Last Judgment will be kinder than our confrontation that day, I pray.

To be sure, there were trouble-free moments and deeds of mine that blotted out these lapses on my record, so that my long-suffering parents kept alive their fervent hope that I would become a good citizen in time. After all, hadn't my father given me the Chinese name of "Peace?" Wasn't "Wo Doy" the diminutive nickname for "Peace" by which I was addressed around the house? Or did they shake their heads and secretly wonder at the incongruity of it?

Fortunately, there was a flip side to my coin. I was a dependable, pious kid who faithfully rode his bike on cold winter mornings to serve mass at the altar. Mother gave me handsome leather gloves at Christmas to protect my hands on those long rides. I ran errands on my bike. I received good grades, won spelling bees and did my homework without prodding.

If any doubts about my integrity still lingered, they were finally wiped away when I turned twelve. I arrived home, following an eighth-grade retreat at school, directed by Fr. Alexis, our much-admired parish priest. I waited for the right moment. Then I blurted out the dramatic announcement that I was a candidate for the seminary. I had decided—as much as a twelve-year-old can decide—that I would become a priest!

Instantly, my reputation was salvaged. The past was forgotten. This erstwhile bad seed was a good seed, after all. Mother was elated, father was not. It was not what he had hoped for; after all, he had built a business that he dreamed one day would incorporate his sons.

Nonetheless, all their years of silent tears and fears were finally resolved. Since a priest carried an aura of nobility and virtue, their son with his checkered past would finally be a source of happiness and pride to them, not misery and shame.

So, having just turned thirteen, I was off to the seminary in the company of a dozen others from my class. My father's initial question: "What does a twelve-year-old know about life?" was soon answered. By year's end, all but two of my companions had awakened to the reality that a life choice is more than fun and games. One by one they took their one-way tickets home.

I stayed, however, through the following twelve years of training. To say I persevered would imply that it was a constant struggle to cling to my life choice, which it was not. Year simply followed upon year, each marked with significant events which seemed quite normal: classmates quit periodically; teachers, some top rate and others so-so, came and went; the routine of studies and play made the days flow by smoothly and swiftly.

What was not routine was my passage into manhood when I turned thirteen. There followed a worrisome, almost frantic period when my conscience was weighed down by the fear of damnation, as I was led to believe. While the hormones in me thrashed and raged wildly, I struggled mightily to tame them under pain of mortal sin and fear of eternal perdition. Add to this my abysmal ignorance or innocence about sexual matters. I was alternately shocked and educated, amused and aroused by the graphic stories and jokes told by some of my more worldly-wise classmates on our long walks.

In 2002 I celebrated fifty years of ordination. In that time I have been a high school teacher and administrator, an associate producer in TV and film, a peripatetic preacher and a retreat house director. My students and audiences have been many. Ultimately, they are the ones who will evaluate my life and ministry and pass judgment on my presence and impact in their lives.

When my family saw me off to the seminary those many years ago, they were relieved and assured that their son and brother would bring honor to them and to the world-at-large as a leader and model of restraint and virtue. And yet my foregoing self-revelation would appear to bury that expectation. It's as if I stand before the reader without clothes.

As a septuagenarian I am well aware of having reached the final turn on life's course. The years of experience have convinced me that I share the common strengths and weaknesses of others. My narrative might well serve as a mirror held up to them as well. Beneath the layers of pretense and false modesty, I am like everyone else, perhaps even worse.

And so, in these remaining years my goal is to accept the challenge "to fight the good fight" to the end, as Paul urged his friend Timothy. (I Tim 6:12) Then what an enormously thrilling and wondrous moment it will be to discover the full answers to life's who, what, when, where, how and why. "No eye has ever seen nor ear heard nor has any mind ever conceived the things that God has prepared for those who love him." (1 Cor 2:9)

"Your children are like your fingers; similar but no two alike."

Chinese Proverb

"To be or not to be, that is the question."
William Shakespeare's Hamlet
"To be all you can be, that is the challenge."
The Gospel

Chisel on Marble

At the Academy of Fine Arts in Florence, Italy, I finally saw it in the "flesh." "It" was the magnificent marble masterpiece of David, the giant-killer, by Michelangelo. Many years back, Fr. Celestine had created in me an appreciation and hunger for the great Renaissance artist's work in our art history class, so that my first trip to Europe was a feast for the eyes and imagination.

Legends surround the statue's creation: how it was carved and fashioned from a castoff hunk of marble, useless because of its odd rectangular shape. But to Michelangelo's visionary eyes the stone held a deep secret. There, hidden within the marble block, was the rippling physique of the young shepherd hero, David, who slew Goliath, the Terror of the Israelites, with a single stone hurled from the sling hanging at his side.

Now that the awesome larger-than-life figure stands majestically on its pedestal, freed from its marble prison, I can easily imagine the finished David expressing gratitude and relief to Michelangelo for liberating him.

In the museum's anterior room, another hunk of marble rests on a pedestal. A human form is only partially emerged, frozen in a crouch, as if locked forever in an enormous struggle to free itself from its stony casing. Its bent posture, straining under the weight on its shoulders, seems to be pleading for release.

It's a male figure, but I think it symbolizes perfectly the struggle of every human being from birth to death, in the process of forming and emerging, striving to reach the outer limits of his or her potential.

Marble stands for permanence, the stuff of gravestones meant to last for the ages. But in the glorious David sculpture, or his tender Pieta and the mighty Moses, Michelangelo shows that even marble can be shaped into marvelous, breathtaking forms so real that they might speak to us at any moment.

When I think of human mind sets, attitudes and tendencies, I am reminded of marble's hardness. Stubbornness, an untamed temper, and habits of laziness — all are like marble that resists the mallet and chisel of self-polish and refinement. When I convince myself that possessions and status replace self-discipline and self-realization, or if I adopt a you-can't-change-me-I-know-it-all hard shell of arrogance and conceit, then I am like the pathetic half-figure locked in that unfinished block of marble. What a waste of a life.

When Luke and Matthew's gospels (Mt. 25:14 & Lk. 19:12) both tell Jesus' story of how a certain important person summoned his servants to entrust his wealth to them in his absence, I am compelled to face up to my own identity and goals. Stripped of all sense of self-importance I am reminded of a basic truth: that what is mine has been given to me—on loan. The Master's point is clear and unavoidable: I was born endowed, gifted, with many or few talents to be used and multiplied in my lifetime. Then at some future point the Master will rightfully ask for an accounting of how resourceful and diligent I have been in the use of his gifts.

While the sum of my raw potential at birth may be five, two or only one talent, it will be more than I can ever fully actualize in my life span. My goal, of course, is to become as completely as possible the person I am capable of becoming — to become whole — or, to use an otherwise religious term, holy.

The joy and pride of a father and mother as they hold their newborn baby ever so tenderly, bursting with hopes for its good health and safety, to enjoy the loftiest mental and creative gifts, and ultimately to attain honor and success - oh, the very best of everything - all this is but a dim reflection of the pride and expectations of my unseen Father God who brought me out of nothing.

To my Father God I am precious and beautiful-not more than anyone else, but not any the less either. Placed mysteriously in this time and place, I am never out of God's sight. My gifts, be they life itself and good health, each of my good thoughts, ideas and skills, all flow from God's infinite treasury of creativity and are entrusted to me to be used productively. This is my Father's dream and wish.

What is even more impressive and somewhat intimidating is to be aware that there is not, nor has there ever been, another person identically endowed as I. I am one of a kind, as is every other person in the world. I have a unique task to accomplish in my lifetime. And while my life may be long or short—and it always seems to be too short—there is always time enough to do what God has created me to do. Others may do what I do and better, but it is my own particular stamp on it which my Father God sees and cherishes.

When I will have actualized all my potential, then I will be fulfilled and genuinely happy. I will be whole or holy in the truest sense. Then I can picture the pride in my Father's heart for my having come up to his expectations and dreams for me.

I cannot allow myself to forget that my talents and potential, such as they are, are not meant to be developed in rivalry and competition with others. Besides being irrelevant, the jealousy they create over another's accomplishments generates ugly resentments and a silly competitiveness that destroys peace.

If, out of envy or ambition, I try to become or to do something beyond my capabilities, I am doomed to failure or at best mediocrity. The truth is, if I am flat-footed rather than fleet-footed, I will always run second or worse. If my voice is coarse and my ear is tin, I will never be operatic. If I am plain looking and not even ugly, I will not be asked to play Romeo. If I cannot add or subtract, I will not work in a bank for long.

On the other hand, why do I witness so much boredom, frustration, stress and anger in my friends and acquaintances? They complain about their bosses, their co-workers, their work place. And the bitterest irony of all is that healthy paychecks do not soften the pain of their day to day struggles.

I have seen too many wonderfully gifted people who are not allowed the opportunity to use their innate, God-given gifts. They are often ignored and passed over by oppressive or blind overseers, silenced, exploited or stomped on. Rather than raise their voices in protest, they have settled for menial, unchallenging tasks that kill by deadening, assembly-line routines. They are bottled up and frustrated. They were meant for greater things. Like the poor bent figure locked forever in that marble block, they are never freed to share their gifts with others.

My supreme goal in life is to be happy. I have found happiness and contentment to be the fruit of fulfillment, that is, becoming what my Father God planned and willed for me when He first brought me out of nothing and endowed me with vast potential. One day I dream how He will welcome me into His loving embrace, pleased with the final work of myself, just as Michelangelo must have admired his masterpiece of David.

The boy Jesus grew in age, wisdom and grace.
(Lk 2:52)

How To Love Myself

The Master gave five talents to one, to another two, to a third one..."
(Mt. 25:15)

Two young men were conversing when I approached. Nothing unusual about that except that they were flat on their backs on separate hospital gurneys, each one's feet pointing at the head of the other, both talking toward the ceiling. The reason, I found, was that both were quadriplegics, paralyzed from the neck down, spines severed. John told how he had been in a van accident, while on a lark with fun-loving buddies. Jim had snapped his spine while high diving.

"Do you feel cheated?" I asked both. " Are you angry at God, the driver or anybody, for what happened to you?"

"Naw," John was brave, "I figure if this is what God wants, it's OK with me." Edifying.

"But what good is your life?" I countered, forcing him to face his deepest, most genuine feelings. "Others have to wash you, feed you, move you, do everything for you."

He blanched. "Wow," he murmured, "that's a heavy question."

"Well, you should find an answer for it," I pressed. "You know, you're around twenty years old, so you've got a long, long life ahead of you."

When I dropped by later, he called, "Hey, I think I've got an answer for you! I wonder if I'm not like this so others can serve me."

"To enable others to serve me." A heavy answer to a heavy question. On the face of it, a seemingly self-centered attitude. On closer look however, it may be one of the most profoundly unselfish, admirable insights possible.

John's self-acceptance enables him to find value in his crippled condition. In a worldly, materialistic climate that evaluates people by their productivity and profitability, John might have been excused for considering himself a burden on others. He might have shriveled up, bitter and resentful, despising those who were to blame for his condition, and worse yet, challenging God for allowing such an unfair twist of fate to befall him.

Put into similar tragic predicaments, other people have been known to withdraw into a shell of self-pity or even to end their miseries by suicide.

In truth, every person is on earth, like John, to be served by others. But the reverse is equally true. Each one is here to be of service and to share with others uniquely personal gifts and strengths.

No one is totally self-sufficient and ruggedly independent. Each one is, like John, limited and handicapped to a degree. Side by side we stand beside others, mutually interdependent, needing each other. I will write; you will read. You need me; I need you. Each time I serve you or you serve me, it is love.

But before I can love you, my neighbor, I must first "love myself." Then, to the degree I love myself, I am to love you, my neighbor. Unrealistic? Unfair? Not in Jesus' view. When asked how to attain the kingdom, he stated flatly, "You must love your neighbor as yourself. Do this and life is yours." (Lk 10:27)

"To love myself" sounds like a bad case of narcissism or vanity. What it really means is that I accept myself as I am, the way the Lord wishes me to be, having created me as I am. On my part I will develop and use my gifts, such as they are. My energies are spent fulfilling my God-given potential.

Nothing that happens is meaningless or useless. There is purpose and value to everything. If the Lord so chooses, even sickness and disability can serve and bring glory to him. It is God's will, God's plan, God's purpose that I serve. Living by this standard brings me a deep sense of fulfillment and peace.

So my newfound friend John found his reason for living by being a patient, outgoing and likeable, enabling others to serve him while truly enjoying his company. Even as I write this, he is serving others and me by inspiring us.

It's not superb human specimens alone who can give glory to God. Even ninety-eight pound weaklings can bring greater glory to God—and frequently do, I'm sure.

To love myself means to bloom and grow, as a flower unfolds and bursts into elegant color and texture, form and fragrance. I am in awe of all the human family's creativity, poured out in an ocean of arts and sciences: infinite forms of music, dance, drama, literature, painting, philosophy, technology, medicine, athletic prowess, capped by the ethereal visions of poets and mystics. These are some of the magnificent outpourings of human potential, bequeathed to a world straining toward fulfillment. Even I, merely a molecule in the human body, am to contribute a distinctive part to the whole.

Jesus often alluded to God-given talents and to the master's disappointment and retribution against lazy defaulters. What I possess is his endowment, loaned to me for a time, to be used in the building of his kingdom on earth. The Creator Father has invested heavily in me. He has high hopes and expectations. He is counting on me.

Will success spoil the artist and high achiever? Yes, if the success is sought for itself, solely to the profit and pride of the achiever. When a celebrity remarks ruefully, "It's more fun getting to the top than being there," I catch a glimpse of the basically self-serving attitude and motive that prompted the striving to reach the top. If that is my ambition, then I can blame and rely only on myself to fend others off who threaten to depose me. Records will forever fall because human potential is virtually unlimited. The summit of perfection I strive after is ever beyond the next horizon.

The mythical top can be reached and shared by everybody, each according to his gifts. I must push myself. I must compete with myself. I alone am responsible for what has been entrusted to me. To love myself doesn't imply "over everybody else." Jealousy often poisons one who is not satisfied with doing one's best and who needs to surpass all others.

God is the source of everyone's gifts, unequally distributed. I stand alone, responsible only for doubling my share, accountable for my record of achievement or failure. Fortunately, unlike many parents, the Lord does not draw comparisons of achievement or performance between his children.

When I truly love myself I will become the finest instrument of greatest use to my Father Creator. I will be better equipped and ready to serve. The entire world will be enriched by my presence and my service.

The incarnation of Jesus Christ is my model for the fulfillment of my potential. In his birth, life, sufferings, death and resurrection, Jesus gave me the pattern of my climb toward self-realization, to the glory of God the Father.

St. Irenaeus enthused, "The glory of God is humans fully alive!" And when I will have brought all my powers together to peak, I will have become whole and holy. Far from pietism and affectation, holiness means to be wholly, successfully human—the way God created me to be.

The darkness flees...
here comes the sun!

"I am the light of the world
anyone who follows me will have
the light of life."
Jn 20:28

The Light of Truth

I once enrolled in a Reality Therapy workshop led by the renowned psychologist William Glasser. Reality, according to Dr. Glasser, is one's situational environment in which life challenges can be transformed into positive, worthwhile results. But some people, unfortunately, find their hurdles too high and difficult to handle. So, by denying the reality of their problem, they will frequently escape into an unreal world of alcohol or drugs, and even affect radical behavioral changes. They will drop out, act crazy or violently. "If I act like a lunatic," they reason, "I won't be held to my responsibilities."

Applying his unique technique called Reality Therapy, Dr. Glasser is reputed to have therapeutically emptied whole wards of social dropouts from veterans' hospitals. During our workshop, we were to test his methodology.

In one role-playing session, an experienced therapist from a state institution volunteered to portray one of her real-life patients. "I'm down in a cave where some huge elephants are threatening to trample me to death," she play-acted, rolling her eyes. The student assigned by Dr. Glasser to solve the case reacted solicitously, "Oh, tell me more about those elephants…"

Abruptly, Dr. Glasser stood up, shouted and pounded his fist, "Cardinal rule number one! You NEVER talk crazy with the crazies! Move over, let me show you how to deal with this. First you make friends to win their confidence – 'Hi, I'm Dr. Glasser. I'm here to help you' - and he held out his hand to the make-believe insane person – 'and you know what? You're crazy as hell…!'"

Brutal. Unflinching. Honest. Direct. Like grabbing someone by the collar and shaking him violently and shouting, "Wake up! Stop this nonsense! Stop wasting your life and everyone else's." It was a verbal slap of truth, hoping to bring the dropout back in touch with reality.

And of course that is what truth is—reality, the way it is. There are no elephants in caves or, for that matter, no dragons, monsters or ghosts. No, there aren't even any bogeymen who used to keep me in line as a kid. Back then my feverish little mind had no difficulty imagining those terrifying specters. Fear paralyzed me. But the truth is, in my seventy-plus years I have yet to encounter my first bogeyman, ghost or demon.

Am I just whistling in the dark? I suppose I am, to a certain extent. After all, my knowledge of all that exists is, to say the least, extremely limited. More than that, I have no absolute certitude that what I accept as true now is in fact true. Beyond that, if I knew everything within the covers of a twenty-volume encyclopedia I still wouldn't know everything there is to know. To complicate matters, when "new and revised" editions are published, it implies that the previous authoritative information has been either amended or expanded.

The amount of data and information school children are expected to assimilate today is twice what I had to learn at their age. Not only that, much of what I learned must now be unlearned. Why? Simply because it was not true, then or now. Was I lied to? Objectively speaking, yes, because it did not conform to reality.

Scientists, theologians, academicians, experts in all fields—and even simple, progressive experience, all are formidable, challenging analysts of today's information and understanding. Debunking is a healthy way of digging out the truth. When I find new insights that contradict accepted "truths" incontrovertibly, then it makes good sense to clear the attic of my mind. And what a welcome, refreshing sensation it brings!

Until the next purging… and the next, ad infinitum. The fundamental truth is that reality is virtually unlimited and inexhaustible. It is most humbling to realize that so much that exists out there is still waiting to be discovered. Like a treasure hunter I can search each long day in a vast storeroom for things both new and old. (Mt. 13:52). Humans will never fathom all there is to know of the vast universe, let alone the secrets and the mysteries of the human body and the microcosmic world around us.

But now, what of the Ultimate Reality—the source and the summary of all that is, the Root of All Being? What of the One who was introduced to me from earliest childhood as God?

I have never had any great difficulty believing in God, the Reality never seen by anyone. And yet my teachers were so sure of what they taught me about God. Is it true that I was created out of nothing to know God and then to love and to serve Him? And why do I speak of God as a He and not a She? Did God give me life to satisfy a divine need, so that if I fail to render due worship, or refuse to honor God and live a sinful life. I will suffer an eternity of hell fire?

Is God really so self-serving? Is God so insecure and deprived that my feeble worship will add its smidgen to his infinite glory? Is this sort of questioning insolent? Ought I to be more circumspect, just in case?

What are the answers? Not any answers, but the truth. Truth is the light that draws all living things to itself. Jesus is the light of the world. He declared: "If you make my word your home you will indeed be my disciples. You will learn the truth and the truth shall set you free." (Jn 8:31-32) Free! From ignorance that generates fear, guilt and anxiety! The reality or truth about God is stunningly beautiful and life giving. To know God as he truly is, is to find total peace and joy.

No wonder St. Paul would exclaim: "Oh, how rich are the depths of God - how deep his wisdom and knowledge - how impossible to penetrate his motives or understand his methods! For who could ever know the mind of the Lord? Who could ever be his counselor? Or who could ever give him anything or lend him anything? All that exists comes from him - all is by him and for him. To God be glory forever. Amen." (Rom 11:33-36)

"I'm behind you, no matter what."
—God

Billions of Blind Mice

Pete is a good friend who has difficulty dealing with diversity of opinions. To disagree with him and the ultraconservative readings on which he feeds himself, along with his daily dose of health food, means you are wrong. Period. He might well have coined the dictum "If I want your opinion, I'll give it to you." While he may be grinning impishly when he declares for the umpteenth time, "I made only one mistake in my life: that's when I thought I was wrong but I wasn't," I think he really means it.

· · · · · · · · ·

Once when Jesus was walking ahead of a noisy crowd of followers, a pathetic, blind beggar named Bartimaeus sat by the roadside, hoping for alms. As the commotion grew louder, he asked and learned that the crowd was tagging along with the well-known Jesus. So he began shouting out, "Jesus, have pity on me!" Some insensitive people in the crowd became annoyed and yelled at the poor beggar, "Oh, keep quiet!"

Instead, the beggar raised his voice even louder, "Have pity on me, Jesus!"

Jesus stopped and said, "Bring that fellow over here." So they went to him and told him, "Hey, get up. He's calling for you. But don't worry. You don't have any reason to be afraid of him!"

"What do you want from me?" Jesus asked.

"Master, I really would like to see," the blind man begged. Without a pause, Jesus said, "All right, go now, it's your unshakable conviction, your faith in my power that has healed you."

Instantly the man's sight was restored, and he jubilantly joined the crowd following Christ. (Mk 10:46-52)

In this very moving story I see myself in the blind Bartimaeus. My very humanness means my vision is limited and, in many ways, totally unseeing. And yet, like my friend Pete, I sometimes don't hesitate to make absolute statements and draw conclusions with unblinking certitude and finality. At times, to bolster my stance, I will lean on the words and official pronouncements of acknowledged authorities, people who are supposed to know. But in the end, as abundant historical evidence shows, we could all be blind mice leading other blind mice.

"Everybody lies" is a truism that is also good cautionary advice. Not that everybody sets out with malicious intent to deceive and mislead. Quite the contrary. The great irony is that people lie in all sincerity because they're blind to the truth and don't know any better. Which is why I have found myself saying and believing things taught to me that do not in fact conform to reality. No reason for alarm. After all, the limited human mind is simply incapable of grasping the vastness of all reality.

The larger question now becomes: Then, why am I—and others as well—so obsessed with always being right? And with such close-minded, bull-headed obstinacy and absolute finality? Rigid intolerance of other views drives wedges of discrimination and even hatred between people different by reason of religion, politics and ethnic cultures.

Why am I not humble and wise enough to preface my statements with an open-ended: "So far as we know…" or "Most evidence points to…" to allow for further insights and investigation?

I suppose I am like everyone else in need of security and stability. I have to be sure. To be on a rocking boat or shaky ground is unnerving. There's nothing more reassuring than good ol' terra firma. As a result, I settle for the notion that, if it's in print, it must be right. Or I assume that the trained experts and authorities in various fields of knowledge who taught me can't be wrong.

Then going beyond the natural sciences, there are those mysteries that transcend all human knowledge: God, life and death and what follows after, sin and its consequences. The darkness enveloping these realities hang over my life like a thick, impenetrable shroud.

All around me are searchers flocking to gurus and sites of visions, looking for final answers that remove all doubt. Now enters the imagination to play seductive tricks and to conjure up visions of monsters and evil spirits. So it was that early map makers routinely sketched in sea monsters beyond the explored oceans with a dire warning: "Here there be dragons."

Long before Galileo's telescope showed our earth to be circling around the sun instead of the sun around it, the earth had always been doing so. People's perception did not alter the reality. While everyone was under the illusion that the sun rose daily in the east and set to the west of a flat earth, the round earth was spinning around the sun. Furthermore, not only was the earth not the center of the universe, but it is only one of other planets circling the sun. Each discovery is but the platform for further probing.

Today I marvel at the scientific efforts to determine if there is life in any form, especially intelligent life, elsewhere out in the infinite vastness of space. That is one more question begging for an answer that will probably yield the truth in the years ahead. Meanwhile, back home here on earth we humans have yet to unravel all the hidden, untapped powers and depths of the mind and body. What is there that we are still blind about? Only God knows.

The crowd told Bartimaeus that Jesus was summoning him and that, more than anything else, he had nothing whatever to fear. The man humbly acknowledged his blindness and asked to be able to see. And Jesus granted it. Can't I learn from this and do the same?

Your faith has saved you, Bartimaeus. You believed that your blindness could be fixed. Being blind didn't keep you from believing that, far beyond any earthly power and material reality, is the supreme reality of a God who watches over and cares for us. We humans have never completely tapped the vast reservoir of all life's mysteries or always been right, and yet we have survived as a race and creation.

If I have learned nothing else, I now understand why it's all right to be wrong and to make mistakes. Erroneous thinking is eventually righted. The human hunger and thirst to know more and more of the truth is insatiable. The human desire to explore and to ask questions is only temporarily satisfied with each new discovery. We can't get enough.

The quest for truth will not stop, so long as God is God, the infinite truth and creator of all reality. There is nothing to be afraid of, so we loudly but humbly cry out with blind Bartimaeus, "Lord, help us to see."

Suegra y Nuera

La Suegra y Nuera

Mother-in-law & Daughter-in-law

The glorious amaryllis with its bell-shaped petals and elegant form bursts into bloom in springtime in scarlets and pinks. Its Spanish nickname is quaintly apt: *Suegra y nuera:* i.e. mother-and daughter-in-law. The nickname fits because the flower bells invariably face away in opposite directions, as though turning their backs to the other.

I suspect most married people can easily identify with the analogy. The tensions between a mother and her daughter-in-law are almost expected and surely not surprising. A mother who has raised her son from infancy knows his tastes and habits well, so she feels that she should share (read, " impose") this knowledge with this new woman in his life. Mother is an authoritative (read, "authoritarian") critic of how food should be prepared and served, since she has prepared his food since he was an infant. Mom is not only qualified; it is her right and duty to offer suggestions and criticize, to the point of interference, if need be, to fend for her own flesh and blood.

While daughter-in-law may be lacking in experience, she has embarked on a long journey of trial and error, gradually discerning the tastes and preferences of her beloved new husband. Until she married, she had acquired her own skills and tastes. Now she will have a lifetime to learn what is satisfying to her spouse and, in partnership with him, to widen their mutual choices. There are, after all, more than a few ways, beyond mother's experience and preference, to prepare an egg or to press a shirt.

Homely as it is, the example of *la suegra y nuera* pointedly illustrates how each person is in fact unique and therefore different in ideas and insights, feelings and attitudes —the whole range of human thought and emotion.

What I perceive or how I see something helps me form my opinions, which then shape my attitudes and ultimately my choices. It goes without saying that my choices will almost certainly clash with another person's choices. But a conflict of choices doesn't mean that those who differ with me are necessarily wrong. They're simply, well, different.

Variety is the spice of life. Uniformity of taste and behavior can become jaded and deadly. To be adventurous and willing to try another recipe can open up a whole new world of tastes and flavors. Experimenting with color, bold and bright, can infuse life into drab and dull rooms and surroundings, not to mention my wardrobe. Mingling with people of different ethnicities and customs can introduce me to a wonderful rainbow mix of new experiences.

La Suegra y Nuera don't have to be inveterate enemies. By bringing them together, providence would have them turn toward each other, see and enjoy their similarities and then explore what gifts the other brings. Be ready for happy surprises.

"It is a difference
of opinion
that makes horse races."

Mark Twain

Love is worth the time it takes to grow.

The Real Miracles

"Jesus went down with them and came to Nazareth, and was obedient to them; he advanced in wisdom, age and grace before God and man." (Lk 2:51-52)

When I was a boy I fancied Jesus doing all kinds of extraordinary God-things using his divine nature. It wasn't hard to imagine him playing with other kids and making mud pies. He would be awesome when he would fashion birds out of mud, clap his hands and watch the birds take off. Why not? Wasn't he God?

And then when he matured and began his preaching to the crowds, Jesus really demonstrated his divine power when he turned plain water into the best wine the people had ever tasted and when he fed five- and ten thousand people with a few fish and loaves of bread, with leftover fragments filling twelve baskets! Then there was the time when he came walking on the water of a stormy lake and hushed the raging waters. He was most in his element when he gave sight to those born blind and injected new life into dead limbs and brought dead people back to life, just to mention some of the more spectacular miracles.

Jesus himself alluded to these as signs and proofs of his divine origin and nature. They're convincing enough for me, even though I've never seen him and have only read about him. I have no problem accepting the fact that he is truly the Son of God in human form, born of Mary the virgin-mother.

But why should it be so remarkable that he performed these wonders? After all, as God he can do things even more marvelous than those recorded in the gospels.

I think that the real miracle, the most stunning aspect in the life of Jesus is that he was like me in all ways - the one exception being that he never sinned.

For Jesus to put on the human condition and everything that implies, now that to me is the real miracle! This means that, as he grew up, Mary and Joseph had to teach and train him to walk, speak, write, read. He learned all the customs and traditions dutifully. He experienced the challenge and tedium behind learning and practicing workaday skills. Joseph had to train him in the use of tools and the craftsmanship of fine carpentry.

To be even more specific, it stirs my soul imagining how Jesus truly experienced every human feeling and sensation: the quenching wetness of cool water when he was thirsty, the exhilaration of diving into the lake with his young friends, the tug of a fish on his line, the taste of a delicious morsel of that fish prepared by his mother, the refreshing stretch and yawn after a nap.

As he grew up in Nazareth, I imagine him as a tanned, handsome lad, lithe and supple as a willow, attractive to and attracted by the pretty girls. I think of him as bright and friendly to everyone, thoughtful and courteous, even a mischievous tease to young and old. Everyone knew him and sought out his company.

And when he worked with his father in the carpenter shop, Jesus was careful and precise, perhaps even a bit clumsy in the beginning. He treated each customer as an important person. When the finished table or chair was ready for delivery, the customer knew that he was getting more than his money's worth in materials, craftsmanship and courtesy.

That Jesus enjoyed the smell of the wood and its smoothness, running his callused hands over its grain and surface, is marvelous to contemplate.

Jesus experienced firsthand all my anxieties, weariness and exhaustion. He thrills with my triumphs and weeps with me over my failures.

He experienced the painful stab of rejection and cried in frustration at being ridiculed.

This means that, as body bags arrive from the front bearing the remains of dead soldiers, he feels the awful pain of the grieving families.

All this was summed up in the single declaration: "The Word was made flesh and lived among us." (Jn 1:14) Jesus, the Son of God, became a fellow human.

Jesus is the Word of God, which is to say, he is the *"I love you"* of God, addressed to all humanity and to the entire universe. God did not create the universe and then abandon it. Rather, Jesus put on our own humanity, thus becoming our big brother, and made it possible for me and all people to become the children of God. *Amazing!"*

My tendency is to think of these down-to-earth details as too grubby and banal for

Jesus, Son of God. But that is precisely the point. They are the very things he chose to identify with by his down-to-earth humanity.

The real miracle in the life of Jesus is that he experienced life exactly the way I do. Incredible!

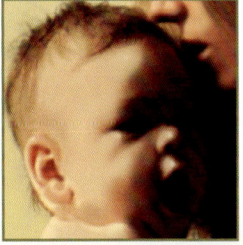

Q: Who is the adopted child?

There Oughtta Be a Law

"There are no illegitimate children – only illegitimate parents." –Judge Leon R. Yankwich

Two battle-toughened Marines were lunching together in the train diner. They were swapping war stories and experiences with colorful language. Abruptly they halted their salty talk when two nuns in full habit entered the car at the far end. With a wink and a nod in the nuns' direction, one Marine whispered: "Let's give 'em the business." His buddy smirked assent.

The two religious women took their table seats across the aisle. After awhile, as the meal was served, one Marine spoke up in a voice the women could easily hear.

"Did I ever tell you, Joe, that my mother wasn't married when I was born?"

"Naw. Is that so?" the partner responded. "Well, how about this? My dad was a priest."

After a long minute, the older nun cleared her throat and addressed the men, "Excuse me, but would one of you two bastards please pass me the salt and pepper?"

Put down? Of course not. The two nuns were too disciplined and pious to resort to that. As a matter of fact, the one asking for the salt and pepper was a professor of literature. No question about it, she was addressing them in a very proper manner, even though they may have flinched at being called bastards.

In the nun's innocence and naiveté, it could have been that she did not sense the delicious irony in her request. (I doubt it.)

A bastard is a perfectly acceptable English word denoting a person who is conceived and born out of wedlock.

Above all, bastard is not a cuss word. Only by social practice has it come to mean someone who is beyond description vile and contemptible.

Beside a local freeway is a huge, painted sign that screams:

"LAND EXTORTION! JAIL THE BASTARDS WHO MAKE LIFE SO HARD!"

The frustration and fury of the farmers (I presume), fighting against the takeover of their lands by developers and city hall, are loud and clear. Their most potent weapon is to express their resentment and hatred with the most contemptuous insult they can muster: BASTARDS!

I think it's time to end this disgusting and despicable practice, so unfair and uncalled-for. There ought to be a law! The use of the term as insult should be universally condemned as scurrilous and evil.

The truth is that I know—and you know—too many wonderful persons who must live with this accident of birth. In no way do they deserve to suffer through life with this indignity. I think of the many innocent children, conceived and born to single parents who, for shame or circumstance, choose not to keep and rear them. At which point, the children begin their life odyssey, as foundlings in public institutions or foster homes. Their most fervent hope is to be adopted into a loving family circle and to live as normal a life as possible thereafter.

Then what must be the stabbing hurt to those born out of wedlock on hearing their status spat out as the vilest insult? Their accident of birth is seared into their consciousness like a brand, a stigma insensitive people keep inflicting, even if unwittingly.

My heart aches for those who must surely spend much of their lives wondering about their origins. Who are my mother and father? Why didn't they want me? Who are my grandparents? Do I have brothers and sisters, uncles, aunts and cousins?

These are the most natural questions any human being would like answered. For those born out of wedlock each question bangs against a blank wall. Disconnected. Rootless, even if taken in and reared in a loving family.

In this context and consideration, I can't see how anyone can be so callous as to use bastard as an epithet. Or to hear someone use it and not express disapproval.

There are probably more persons around us born out of wedlock than we know.

Life is a most precious gift from God, who is the ultimate source of all life. How I have received it, whether from loving parents or from someone who has brought me into the world without the benefit of marriage, is really irrelevant.

I am a child of God, destined to live forever. So I will live my life to the full, always bearing in mind the magnificent opportunity that is mine to make the world more beautiful by my presence in it—yes, even by calling others' attention to stamp out the use of a word so often spewed out as an ugly insult.

A: Each delightful child is an adoptee.

Bees are too busy for beauty.

God Rested. God *Rested?!*

"And on the seventh day God rested..." (Gen 2:2)

Shame on me for having poked fun at that scriptural line. I've joked at times about the absurdity of God getting so pooped from six hard days of creation, he had to take a rest.

As if that weren't enough, God followed up by imposing a strict law on all his creatures to do likewise. Hence, the Sabbath rest. Nor was it negotiable. For a catholic, to rest from servile labor bound under pain of mortal sin. Meaning that, if you did strenuous work on Sunday and died unrepentant, you could burn in hell forever. But oddly, you could crack your brains while burning the midnight oil for, say, an exam but you weren't allowed to dig a ditch in the yard.

When I was a boy, there was no shopping on Sunday and stores were closed. While Mom could never do the laundry on Sunday, she'd spend most of the day cooking up elaborate Chinese dinners.

Today malls bustle with shoppers on Sundays and people do their wash at home or at the laundromat without qualms. And people mow lawns and dig ditches with impunity. Clearly, the notion of rest or else live-in-danger-of-losing-your-soul no longer prevails.

I learned early on that "Idleness is the devil's workshop." Translated, that means that busyness is the ideal. Copy the busy bee and industrious ant. Repeat often: "I never take a day off," "I sleep only five hours a night.," "A vacation? I haven't taken one in years." "There's so much to do…"

The typical modern person is torn between the urgency to attack and to complete a monstrous load of agenda that never diminishes. And most ironically, the value of the obligatory burdens has little to do with the worker burdened with the task of accomplishing them—other than the paycheck. How many there are who, if it weren't for the salary, would run from their jobs with no regrets, so much do they detest the unfulfilling work.

The symptoms of this lifestyle are all about us: anxiety, alcoholism, stress, headaches, workaholism, heart attacks, sleeplessness. Never in history have so many been forced to avail themselves of psychological therapists and psychiatrists for relief.

Life's brevity hassles me with pressure and guilt. After over fifty years of ministry, I admit there is so much more I would like to accomplish before I close the books. But are these goals self-imposed or are they God-given? This reminds me of a witty card my sister sent for my birthday: "God has assigned me certain goals I am to reach in my lifetime. Right now I'm so far behind I'm never going to die."

Looked at with proper perspective, I'll never be able to accomplish all I would like to do, but I know I have all the time I need to do what God would have me do.

· · · · · · · · ·

God rested. Such a pure, simple statement. God rested, not because God was exhausted. Following each stage of creation: the skies and heavenly diamonds he scattered across the firmament, the earth mother and her infinite variety of minerals, plants, animals and humans, God rested, that is, he stood back and, like any artist, looked it over. And with each step of creation "God saw how good it was." I can even picture God breathing in the sweet fragrances of orange blossoms and jasmine, savoring flavors (more than 31), feeling textures and marveling at the glorious array of rainbow colors and then, chuckling in muted thunder, declaring, "O, that's good. I like it!"

I think that's why Jesus urged, "Take some time to look at the flowers. Feel them, pick them, smell them. Squeeze their essence into exotic perfumes. They're here and gone by tomorrow. Yet they are so exquisite, no man-made fabric can match a single petal of a bloom. (Lk 12:27)

Look at them. Contemplate them, their marvelous shapes and hues. Where does such delicate design come from? And why so many varieties? A botanist studies such questions and explains how bees, birds, insects and flowers collaborate, symbiotically assisting each other in reproduction and providing nourishment.

Somewhere along this divine scheme, any intelligent being can behold the splendor of beauty spread before him or her and realize, "This has been done for me. How much love an unseen designer has for me! How blind I have been for most of my life. I have eyes but have not seen."

And it's all because I haven't taken the time. I must learn to rest, stand back and look at what surrounds me. The song of the mockingbird and nightingale to entertain me. The cat curled and purring in my lap and the affectionate dog licking my hand. The warm sun and cool breezes that comfort me. The adorable child with her arms wrapped around me. The soothing voice of a friend sharing a humorous moment with me. The play of twilight on the mountains and the billowy clouds sailing across the sky. Mine is the freedom to live and choose as a carefree child of God.

"Ora et labora" was St. Benedict's adage to his monks. "Pray and work" expressed the ideal of monastic living. At the risk of offending my Benedictine friends, I would suggest a third element that meets and rounds out basic human needs. Missing are rest and play. Asceticism developed to the exclusion of physical release and leisure. Religion became joyless. Indulging in fun and pleasure was considered weakness and must be avoided.

But it was by putting aside the work and duties of the week that I would recharge my body and spirit by relaxation and exercise. By thus maintaining a balance of each facet of my humanity, I would become whole or holistic. Even better, holy.

When Jesus paid a visit to his dear friends, Martha and Mary, this very subject arose. Mary sat with Jesus and chatted; Martha hustled around the kitchen, fixing the meal. She was annoyed and complained that Mary wasn't helping. Rather than siding with Martha, Jesus defended Mary who had chosen "the better part." He was emphasizing the beauty and importance of simple presence to another (Lk 10:41).

Pray, Work, Rest/Play—each in proportion. "All work and no play make Jack a dull boy," as everyone knows. But, as *Integrity* magazine once printed, "All play and no work make Jack a dumb jerk."

My first visit overseas to Spain gave me a surprise each midday. Whole cities came to a standstill: stores closed, windows shuttered, sidewalks cleared, tourist sites locked, with only a few window shoppers (probably Americans) wandering about peering at displays. Ah, the wonderful siesta break!

"How beautiful it is to do nothing and then to rest afterwards." – Spanish Proverb.

Ummmm. Pardon me. I think I'm ready for a catnap…

Nephw Mark, Down's Syndrome boy, has enriched the world with love and affection for thirty-five years... ...and counting.

The Beautiful Leper

A leper approached Jesus and pleaded on his knees: "If you want to, you can cure me." Feeling sorry for him, Jesus stretched out his hand and touched him. "Of course I want to!" Jesus said, "Be cured!" The leprosy left him instantly and he was cured (Mk 1:40)

The ho-hum manner in which St. Mark relates this marvelous incident in Jesus' life is unfortunate. Jesus comes across as a completely predictable miracle-worker; you know he's going to cure the man. It's automatic. But aren't there important details St. Mark might have included between the lines that would reveal a more authentic and real Jesus?

What I mean, for instance, is how hideous the disease of leprosy is: where there once were a nose, ears, fingers, toes that have lost all sensation, there are now oozing abscesses and gaping holes The cartilage of the body has died and decayed. Even the skull can become transparent, so that the brain can be seen pulsating. It is a distressingly ugly sight. Didn't Jesus recoil at this ghastly sight and maybe stifle an urge to vomit?

Adding to a leper's misery was the widespread belief that his awful blight was the result of an angry God's vengeance, implying that the guilty victim had broken laws (sinned) and was now reaping his just punishment. By law then, the victim was shunned and ostracized, run out of town. For him to touch someone healthy would contaminate that person, so normal social contact was strictly forbidden.

It's clear that a leper was a scriptural figure of a damned soul, despised and condemned to a hopeless life beyond redemption.

As I reflect on these details, all assumed in Mark's matter-of-fact narrative, I'm compelled to find answers to large questions. Wasn't Jesus the least bit horrified and repelled by the sight of this hideous creature in his way? Didn't the religious prohibitions he was trained to follow make him pause and arm him with good reasons to send the man packing? Any number of legitimate reasons could have justified Jesus to ignore the leper's pathetic plea. In fact, the leper left him free to refuse: "If you want to…"

I'm convinced that Jesus instinctively backed away, stifling an urge to retch.

If not, then the story has little or no meaning to me. If Jesus is an insensitive automaton lacking normal human feelings, then he wasn't human. The whole story would then be about a superman and have no relevance to me. What would be the point of it?

What is presumed in the story is that Jesus must have experienced normal human reactions of revulsion and horror, no question about it. But the power of the incident is that he must have had to stifle his disgust and force himself to look at the wretched man, even to "touch" him, thereby violating the cold, impersonal legal prohibition. Beyond that, I would even say the "touch" of Jesus was more a hug of the poor man who hadn't felt the warmth of human touch in years. Lovingly, Jesus must have run his hand over the diseased parts, simultaneously healing him. All the while, Jesus could be heard muttering, "You poor thing…how sad…"

I remember as a child asking whether Jesus ever laughed and being told of course not, that it was beneath him. Later, I came across various references in books where authors and scholars strained mightily to identify scriptural passages when Jesus must have laughed.

Why has it been so difficult to associate Jesus with normal human reactions and experiences? It must be that human self-esteem is stricken with inferiority. Ordinary human feelings and reactions cannot be worthy of Jesus, the Son of God.

But that is the Good News - that, in spite of human ordinariness, the Word of God took on a human nature, so lifting it high and divinizing it, making it worthy of God!

"The Word was made flesh." (Jn 1:14) Therein lies the dignity and grandeur of being human.

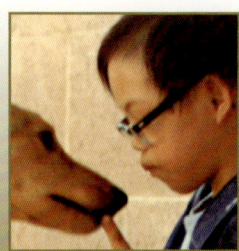

Besides a frog, what if the princess kissed a *skunk?*

Rain or shine, I'll stand by you.

My Treasure

"A friend is a friend always" (Prov.17:17)

My friend shares the seasons of my life, celebrates our good times together, supports me in bad times and walks beside me through the years.

In a cozy garden nook on a warm sunny day, I let my mind and memory roam in reverie. This day I played a little game of calling up some of the happy happenings that had colored my days, like rainbow bubbles floating by. Amazingly, they kept coming and coming, each brushing aside the previous one, eager to be counted. I recalled kind things that were done to me and for me, most of them unexpected, delightful gifts. I was, as we say, counting my blessings. Let me share some of them with you.

Over the week a "ton" of congratulatory letters and gifts arrived from well-wishers on my 50th anniversary of ordination. It tickled me to put a face on each message and recalling happy times shared with each writer.

Eight baskets (count 'em) of glorious yellow, pink and red begonias and a huge basket of red roses greeted me at my door!

My first trip to Bangkok happened - all expenses paid - because a family invited me to officiate at their son's wedding to a Thai bride.

A box arrived from out of state via air express. Its contents? A mouth-watering rum cake soaked in it.

The first glossy issue of a magazine devoted to flowers, birds and butterflies arrived, a gift from one who knows my love for these gorgeous creations.

A person whose mother's funeral I conducted sent a beautiful note of appreciation for helping her deal with "the saddest day of my life."

A highly informed biologist invited me to tour exquisite botanical gardens, our mutual interest, while explaining technical, scientific questions patiently and clearly.

Someone called to inform me that he had spoken up and actually written a letter in my defense to a higher authority against rude and unfair criticisms.

Someone offered to assist me in any way, financially or materially, by underwriting my pet projects.

While I was convalescing in the hospital from heart surgery, a visitor brought flowers and treats daily to ease and shorten the long days.

Using their extremely skillful hands to perform their medical magic on my heart, some of my doctors cared for me gratis.

A concerned person regularly "forces" me to eat well and accompanies me on frequent, hard and demanding walks so I will regain my strength and endurance.

A person who shares my interest in opera, theater, choral and instrumental concerts often invites me as a guest.

A devoted teacher of teenagers who always speaks positively of them, reminding me of my own happy, fulfilling period as a high school teacher and administrator.

A driver on a crowded freeway courteously blinked his lights for me to enter from the on-ramp, followed by a friendly wave.

When I fumbled for a few pennies to pay the tax, a clerk dismissed it with a kind, "That's all right. Don't worry, I can make up for it."

Someone advised me that my breath was offensive and had the courage to suggest how I might remedy it.

A reader of all the foregoing might pass it off as inconsequential, "much ado about nothing." In fact, they are acts of friendship that have colored my life bright green and yellow. I associate "friendly" with a small sign on a narrow rural road that urges, "Drive friendly." Be considerate. Be gentle. Don't be careless and selfish. Look out for the children at play. Wave and smile to those you pass. Turn what may be a glum day for a passing stranger into a sunny one. Courtesy is contagious, so why not start an epidemic?

My list is a compilation of friendly actions of many people. Is it possible that most or all of their actions could have been done by only one person? I think so. In fact, I know so, because nearly all of them, and so many more I don't recall, are done quite regularly by one very special person in my life. That person is my friend.

Without any qualification, my friend is my life's most precious treasure. Again and again, I praise and thank God for so wonderful a gift: someone who truly cares for me, anticipating and providing for my needs and who will stop at nothing to provide for my well-being, asking nothing in return. I spontaneously seek out and confide in my friend, convinced that what is shared is a trust that will never be betrayed. I know without the least doubt that in this person friendship and loyalty are one and the same.

Friendship is a warm blanket of comfort and security in which I can wrap myself during conflict and struggle. My friend lends a sympathetic ear to my travails and comforts me when I am afflicted by grief. When I embark on a new endeavor I can always count on my friend for honest analysis, advice and support. When I am underway my friend stands by me with encouragement and honest criticism through the ups and downs of any undertaking. If I veer off course or become distracted, my friend rouses me and straightens me out.

My friend is the first one with whom I want to share any news, whether good or bad. Our playful teasing of each other serves to bond us, and we vie with each other in the sharing of jokes and amusing stories. Good humor and laughter fill our days together with pleasure and happy memories. We live by the rule: what's mine is yours; what's yours is mine.

Pity the person who goes through life without such a true friend. Now if the profound relationship between me and my friend is a pearl, precious beyond price, then what a staggering revelation it is to picture Jesus looking into my eyes and declaring without qualification, "You are my friend; I have revealed and shared with you everything I have learned from my Father. You are my friend when you love others, just as I have loved you…"

 "And I will soon show to you and to everyone, there is no greater love than to lay down your life for your friend. I refuse to call you a servant, because a servant doesn't know the master's business. I have shared all of this so that you can share in my own infinite joy, and then, my beloved friend, your joy will be complete." (Jn 15:10-15)

Superior Footwear Company
Assisi, Italia

il signore Giovanni Battista Benvenuto
Luigi Corona della Robbia
Presidente e CEO

Success
(The Shoemaker of Assisi)

    Strolling along a cobblestone side street somewhere in the hamlet of Assisi in Italy one day, I came upon a scene that might have been a living painting. It was a doorway in an old stone wall covered with fragments of broken stucco. Inside was a middle-aged man, a shoemaker crafting a shoe. He looked up at me and smiled. We exchanged "Buon Giornos" and with the help of hand-signals I asked if I might take his picture. He readily agreed with a smile. And so, on the facing page I present to you the distinguished president and owner of Superior Shoe Company.

    With a stretch of the imagination, the setting of this scene could well be the luxurious office suite of a corporate CEO in any of the world's major cities. The one important difference would be the contentment in the face of my shoemaker friend. His obvious satisfaction is beyond purchase. His skill was important to someone whose foot measurements he had taken and for whom he now proceeded to build comfortable custom shoes. He didn't have a warehouse filled with countless unsold pairs gathering dust. So long as he awoke each morning with an unfinished pair of shoes to work on that day, there was no fear of an idle, wasted day. So he could smile with contentment. He could close shop at any time and return home when he so chose. He wouldn't dream of setting up another shop in a neighboring town to make more money. Life was good.

    Don Giovanni Battista had often seen glossy magazines featuring articles and photos of company presidents in their lavish office suites, staffed by high fashion secretaries. He read how their companies distributed their products worldwide and employed thousands of employees. Their profits were in figures he couldn't even imagine.

The thought entered his mind that, by taking on a few more customers and working several hours more each day, he could double his income. By saving his profits he would eventually be able to bring in a partner and expand his business beyond the confines of his village. The reputation of his shoes would spread rapidly until the demand forced him to build a factory and hire dozens, maybe even hundreds of workers to fill the orders. Why not?

Don Giovanni Battista laughed. His seductive daydream ignored the total picture. This wise man could see beyond the glitter of riches and fame, the cost in terms of his loss of leisure and contentment. He was smart enough to know that a partnership, while appealing at first sight, often fails because of a difference in goals and values. The same applied to the workers whose workmanship would not always come up to his standards.

But realistically, why expand? Why did he need anything more than what he already had? His customers were all local friends who kept coming for his well-made shoes.

They always dropped by for their customary chats and sometimes even to discuss their family matters. He was almost a surrogate confessor-counselor for the local pastor.

Now and then his thoughts carried him back to that carpenter shop in Nazareth where both Joseph and Jesus built assorted furniture pieces. He was sure that they would not simply make chairs that were then piled up in a warehouse. Most probably items were made in response to a particular customer's need. There was a lot of attention given to detail to match the desires of the buyer.

It would have been impossible for Joseph and Jesus to pass along something that was not the best they could produce of the best materials. Their customers left happy and satisfied, absolutely convinced that they had received exactly what they had hoped for. Besides that it had not been an impersonal buying and selling exchange. Rather, it was in a real way, a favor done for a trusting friend.

Why, wondered Don Giovanni Battista, can't that be the case in every exchange between persons? Because, he finally concluded, that was why he was so satisfied with his profession and loved, actually loved, to come to work each day. Yes, life was good. And he breathed a little prayer of gratitude to God for having given him his calling as the president and owner of Superior Shoe Company.

Those we admire the most, we imitate.
I like your style.

Foxes don't get into fixes like this. I'm sorry.

The Beast with Seven Heads

"A huge red dragon appeared which had seven heads…"
(Rev 12:3)

When I was only a few weeks old my parents dutifully carried me to St. Mary's to be baptized. They had been taught to believe that if I were to die without baptism I would be consigned to limbo (wherever that is) for all of eternity. There in limbo all of my baby needs would be supplied everlastingly, but I would never know the joy of being with God in heaven.

That was the price of being born, a phenomenon accompanied by the stigma and burden of the Original Sin, traceable to the first parents, Adam and Eve. Just imagine, an innocent baby, considered not-so-innocent, born through no choice of its own, but who "inherits" some sin or stain which deprives it of everlasting happiness. However, one life preserver remained: baptismal waters would lift the stain, and a newborn baby would thus be reborn as a child of God. Without that ritual a baby is a helpless spiritual orphan awaiting adoption, if it is so fortunate.

It makes more sense to me to think of birth as the hand of God delivering a magnificent new creation, not stained but filled with enormous possibilities and perfectible. The tiny person is given a lifetime opportunity to unwrap, as it were, the vast trove of talents and gifts endowed by the Creator-God.

After all, Original Sin doesn't fit the concept or nature of a sin - that is, a choice to do some wrong or harmful thing. Clearly, I for one knew I wasn't able to choose to do anything, good or bad, while awaiting birth.

It makes more sense to me to think of Original Sin as the innate propensity in every human to be egotistical and selfish. As I experience in myself and observe in others, often at my expense, self-centeredness is a dragon-beast with seven heads, lurking in every heart. The heads rear up all through life in varying forms and degrees, at times predictably, at other times surprisingly, as Pride, Avarice, Envy, Anger, Lust, Gluttony and Sloth.

Even though I learned these as the Seven Capital Sins, they are not actual sins at all but the tenacious tendencies within me to act in self-centered ways that cause so much hurt and harm.

But the worst, unhappy fact is that the multi-headed dragon in me can't be slain or exterminated. Baptism failed to do it. So I tend to dismiss it with a casual "nobody's perfect" shrug.

The seven-headed beast inside of me is indestructible; it can only be trussed up, caged and controlled through tireless vigilance and self-discipline.

When Jesus was dragged through the mock trial before his crucifixion, he was overwhelmed with fear and dread in the olive grove. Drenched in bloody sweat he stumbled to his stalwart apostles, only to find them sound asleep, not standing guard and praying, as he had pleaded. Ever so sadly, he explained away their drowsiness with, "The spirit is willing, but the flesh is weak" (Mt 26:41)

St. Paul groaned over his own personal struggle, which mirrors my own so well: "I cannot understand my own behavior. I fail to carry out the things I want to do, and I find myself doing the very things I hate. This seems to be the rule, that every single time that I want to be good, it is something evil that comes to hand." (Rom 7:15)

If this image of a seven-headed dragon fits the Original Sin, then to believe that baptism eliminates it is to ignore and deny the challenges of life and living. This denial is a form of blindness that lulls me into a false sense of security and complacency.

From the very beginning, parents must face endless tests of motivating and training Dick and Jane not to be selfish and spoiled. The "Don'ts" of child-rearing are without end: don't brag and show off, don't be impolite, don't be greedy, don't fight, don't eat too much, don't be disrespectful, don't forget to study, don't be jealous, don't be lazy, don't be extravagant, don't be wasteful, don't hurt anybody, don't interrupt, etc., etc. In a word, don't be selfish.

Conversely, the "Do's" or positive counsels of parents and teachers to children are just as difficult to assimilate into life habits to counter selfish traits: Do share with others, be thoughtful, be generous, be respectful, be courteous, be kind, be forgiving, be cheerful, be humble, be modest, be thrifty, be on time, be neat, be dependable, be considerate, be orderly, be clean, etc., etc.

Brats screaming in public places and naughty, insolent, mouthy and sassy children testify to the parents' difficulty and failure in their primary duty of training offspring to be unselfish. The larger tragedy is that these obnoxious children often carry into their adulthood these same selfish attitudes and traits, by now set into intractable, hardened habits.

I am not the least bit surprised that the lifestyles of the rich and the famous become the fantasy and enviable paradigm of so many. Inflated, flamboyant celebrity, however superficial, too often arrives dripping with excess, flaunted arrogantly. It's nauseating to hear someone proclaim shamelessly "I deserve it" and then proceed to squander extravagantly.

If only there were a simple, inescapable way to be convinced that sharing my gifts and goods, not amassing or wasting them, is the key to the happiness that is so desirable but so elusive in life.

St. Paul minces no words: "When self-indulgence is at work the results are obvious: fornication, gross indecency and sexual irresponsibility; idolatry and sorcery; feuds and wrangling, jealousy, bad temper and quarrels; factions, envy, drunkenness, orgies and similar things..." (Gal 5:19-21)

From the very beginning, as Scripture affirms, pride and self-centeredness have been the downfall of God's creatures. Lucifer is portrayed as being so conceited he sought to rival God. The very idea of a creature imagining itself to be as great or greater than the Creator is indescribably sad and ridiculous, and, yes, even laughable. And yet Lucifer personifies an ego bloated with self-importance.

If I am so wrapped up in myself, I will use any means to enhance my status. I must be *numero uno* so I will discredit and destroy any rival who would challenge my supremacy. I love and despise the fawning of underlings and kowtowing of inferiors who look up to me. I spare no expense on luxurious living, since I have earned my status through my own genius and ambition. It's all mine. With my wealth and power I can acquire whatever I want, and my wants happen to be insatiable. Don't I deserve it? Isn't it mine to use as I wish? And if I don't like you I'll get rid of you. I owe you nothing. You are as disposable as used tissue. I can replace you or anything I choose, anytime I please.

It's shocking how examples of such arrogance have become commonplace in today's ego-feeding world. It's the stuff of slick publications and other mass media. More ironic and distressing is how it feeds the fires of pride and envy in others less prominent but equally avaricious and selfish.

When I see and hear of the horrific acts of human brutality to one another in each day's news—the sordid acts of rape and torture, the degrading of women and even small children, the callous uprooting and eviction of families—and trace such barbaric behavior to the perpetrators, I realize that it is the dragon beast let loose upon the land.

It occurs to me that, in another circumstance, I myself could well be responsible for such monstrous deeds.

My baptism surely did not destroy the dragon beast lurking inside of me. But baptism brought me into the company of others who share the same struggle of containing the beast. Should I fail I know I will find forgiveness and strength from that company of others to rise up again to continue the struggle. I draw comfort from knowing that I am not alone. And, because God is near, I know I can succeed. The Lord says: "My grace is enough for you; my power is best in weakness…" (2 Cor 12:9)

Baptism is far more than a shield against my wrong tendencies. It has empowered and dispatched me to make the world a better place by word and action. What a great responsibility and privilege to have been chosen to work hand in hand with the Spirit of God's love in so noble a venture. "You have not chosen me; no, I have chosen you…". (Jn 15:16)

Seize the challenge...and the impossible becomes *possible!*

*With your love surrounding me...
my life is awesome.*

The Secret That Shouldn't Be

As a young kid I always noticed on the masthead of the comics page a small impish figure - it was Puck, (I know now) - with a banner in his hand. It read "What fools these mortals be." I have to admit that I didn't really grasp its true relevance back then. But it's now clear that the antics, idiocies and pratfalls of the cartoon characters back then, and now, are so funny because they reflect real life and human behavior.

By the time he began speaking publicly, Jesus could well have been a cartoonist with a strip entitled: "What fools these mortals be!" He had spent his private life observing the ridiculous pretenses and hypocrisy of religious leaders, the cold-heartedness of the rich and powerful, the widespread ignorance surrounding illness and mental/physical defects, the mistreatment of strangers and the unfortunate. And so much more.

While lampooning is an effective tool to draw attention to human foibles and malice, Jesus addressed problems head-on, confronting the pompous pretenders directly, much to their guilty discomfort. But rather than humbly examining the validity of his indictments, the accused arrogantly chose to deny the truth of his charges. Instead they plotted to destroy him. Their silly ploy is a typical example of how proud, stiff-necked scoundrels make futile attempts to hide from the truth.

The large crowds that trailed after Jesus were by and large sincere and open-minded, eager to learn from the Master. And he appreciated their childlike openness and fed them lavishly with soul food as well as with bread, fish and the best wine they ever tasted. His teachings came forth gently and compassionately, unlike the scolding harangues of righteous preachers who themselves have so often been found severely wanting.

They came from every direction, the lame, the sick and the simply hungry and thirsty, and he healed and fed them. Beyond full bellies their yearning was for more: the satisfaction that they all craved to fulfill their lives. So Jesus fed them.

In answer to their most profound question: "How can I find happiness?" Jesus gave them the formula. "How happy are the poor in spirit," he said, "the Kingdom of heaven belongs to them." As simple as that. That simple declaration contains the whole meaning, purpose and goal of life. I have pondered long and hard on its meaning and profound sense.

I remember how it was Lucifer's pride and self-importance lusting to equal and perhaps, while he was at it, even to surpass God's glory and greatness.

Now here's an irony. To be like God is, to be honest, my own deepest desire and highest aspiration. But the critical sticking point is that God is far from egocentric, conceited and greedy.

God is in reality a humble God, so self-effacing that no mere creature has ever seen God face-to-face and lived to tell about it. Yet I am convinced that I see God in muted forms throughout the universe: in the awesome trillions of stars in the trillions of galaxies, in the mighty majesty of mountains and tumbling streams and rivers, the fragrance of flowers, the sweet flavor of fruits, the fleet beauty of beasts.

The wondrous charm and grace of women, men and children ad infinitum are all the gifts of an incredibly generous God.

God is Love. Love is lavish. Love is free and asks nothing in return. Love expends itself and renews itself. Love never ends. Love always forgives. Love is patient. Love is kind. Love does not think of itself, but is always concerned about the well being of those it loves.

God is "poor in spirit." This means that God has everything, yet clings to nothing. God possesses all the glory that is possible. God's grandeur cannot be diminished; it cannot be increased. It simply is. That is why I am able to say that I am God-like, because I share in the grandeur that is God. It's God's gift to me and to everyone else who is or has been - for now and for all eternity!

I am made in the image of God. I will be like God when I, too, am "poor in spirit." God is infinitely happy, and I, too, will be happy only when I am "poor in spirit," not greedy, not proud, not self-centered, but generous, kind, thoughtful and ever-sharing. God has invested his talents and gifts in me, not for my self-glory and conceit, but to be used in the service of others. As much as I give away, so much will I receive in return. It's the way love works. "Give, and there will be gifts for you: a full measure, pressed down, shaken together, and spilling over, will be poured into your lap; because the amount you measure out is the amount you will be given back. Be compassionate as your Father is compassionate. Grant pardon, and you will be pardoned." (Lk 6:36-38)

And how do I know this? Because it emulates the life, actions and behavior of Jesus who was and is the presence of God among us. "His dignity was divine, yet he did not cling to his equality with God but emptied himself to assume the condition of a slave!" (Phil 2:6-7) Don't ask me how it's possible that Jesus could empty himself of his infinite Godness, but there it is in St. Paul's own words, even to the point of laying down his life by the most degrading execution imaginable: nailed to a cross. Do I need to explain "poverty of spirit" any further?

He continued to encourage his eager listeners, listing the corollaries that flow from being poor in spirit. "How happy are the gentle—the kind and nurturing; earth will be their inheritance. How happy are those who mourn; they will be comforted—here in life by others who love them and surely in the life hereafter by God who is Love. How happy are those who hunger and thirst for what is right; they will be satisfied—for Love will eventually triumph and make all things new again. How happy those who are merciful; they will receive mercy—for Love repays itself. Happy are the pure in heart; they shall see God—for lust is controlled and Love treats another with reverence and respect. Happy are the peacemakers; they shall be called the children of God—for Love pardons and restores harmony and right. Happy are those who are persecuted in the cause of right; theirs is the kingdom of heaven—the state of freedom and equality for all God's people who struggle to establish Love's reign in the hearts of all. (Mt 5:1-12)

As I spell out and reflect on this gentle teaching of Jesus on the hillside, it occurs to me that, remarkably, these are the unselfish antidotes to the Seven Heads of the Beast!

He does not engage in a tirade against the prevailing corrupt behavior and arrogance but simply reveals to his listeners the recipe for attaining happiness. For it is happiness that is the missing ingredient in most lives squandered in a greedy, mad scramble for power and possessions.

Why haven't I heard more of this Jesus formula for finding peace and happiness in life? I wonder if it's because the Beatitudes are treated and casually dismissed as mere suggestive advice rather than commandments? Must I be ordered to do something under threat of damnation before I will follow it? Am I still reacting to the gospel teachings like a slave under the lash? The Good News of the gospel Beatitudes is the gentle Jesus way of learning how to live a full, rewarding life in joyful freedom.

It's time to lift the wraps off the secret—the secret that never was meant to be.

"Let me do that for you, dad."
John Chow, cancer survivor since one year old.

Let Me Do It For You

I heard that the Pope was returning to his limousine one day when he felt the urge to drive instead of being driven. So he told the chauffeur to sit in the back as he climbed into the driver's seat. It was so exhilarating to be at the wheel again. But the ride was so smooth that he was up to ninety without realizing it. Oh, oh. The flashing lights of a highway cruiser behind quickly told him. The Pope pulled over, feeling very naughty.

The officer approached, gulped and excused himself as he went back to his cruiser. He contacted headquarters. He needed the advice of his commander.

"Sir, I've got this really important guy who was going ninety. What shall I do?"

"Well, who is it—the mayor?"

"Oh, no. Much more important than that."

"Is it the governor?"

"A lot more important…"

Impatiently, the commander now raised his voice and shouted improbably, "Is it the president?"

"No, no," the officer answered lamely, "All I know is he's got the Pope driving him."

· · · · · · · · ·

The story is funny, I think, because Popes don't drive other people. Custom and protocol don't allow it. It's beneath their dignity. Or so we're accustomed to think.

Yet interestingly, Popes sign off their official statements with *"Servus servorum Dei"* –*"Servant of the servants of God."* But I doubt that most think of the Pope as a servant. It's demeaning.

The human tendency is to elevate VIPs' to a level above ordinary mortals. Royals and rulers of every stripe bask in the glow of honor and privilege. Nothing is too good for them.

The life of Jesus ought to have changed that way of thinking and behaving. I know him as the Son of God who spent his life on earth teaching, healing, feeding and befriending. And then he capped it all when he did an unheard of thing.

This was the night of the Great Passover, commemorating God's deliverance of his people from bondage. Jesus and his apostles were in an upper room to observe the feast. The Master was unusually somber.

"How I've longed for this moment to be with you," he had said (Lk.22:15).

And then followed the staggering announcement that the Passover bread and wine were in fact his very own body and blood to be consumed as spiritual food and drink.

This dramatic act was to become the signature action of all his followers for all ages in memory of him and his total self-immolation that soon followed on the cross.

Each time I celebrate the Mass I am reminded that, in some magnificent, indescribable way I was included in that selfless act of Jesus to cancel my indebtedness to God for my wrongs and those of all others.

Jesus suddenly rose from the dining couch at the Passover meal. The apostles watched with mouths agape as the Master drew a basin of water, tied an apron around his waist, knelt at the feet of each one and proceeded to wash their dusty feet!

What's going on here?! Only servants and slaves rendered this kind of service. But this is the Master abasing himself before their eyes!

As the surreal scene unfolded in slow motion, each embarrassed apostle reluctantly submitted in disbelief. Peter, meantime, lay shaking his head and grousing protestations, until Jesus finally reached him with the basin and towel.

"Oh, no," Peter fairly shouted in his blustery way, "you wash my feet? I won't let you, Master." And he pulled himself away half-angry and righteous.

Jesus sighed and explained patiently, "Do you know what, Peter? If you won't let me wash your feet, you can't have any part of my kingdom."

Still thinking of the "kingdom" as his dream of a political realm of power and prominence and, above all, how he had already been singled out to be its very foundation, Peter quickly rethought his stubborn refusal to submit.

"Oh, well, in that case, don't stop with my feet. Wash me top to bottom," he surrendered meekly.

Having washed the apostles' feet, Jesus asked, "Do you understand what I've just done?" They all nodded affirmatively, although not really comprehending.

"I have tried so often to teach you a fundamental truth: that true greatness lies in a person's willingness to serve others, not in dominating them. Now you have seen me, your Master, who I surely am, wash your feet. That is the way it is in my kingdom, the opposite of glory-seeking and the lust for power. So if I, your Lord and Master, have washed your feet, you should wash each other's feet. Do you understand that?" (Jn 13:1-20)

The light of comprehension seemed finally to dawn on their mindset. But down the centuries, even among those who profess to follow in the footsteps of the disciples, the stunning lesson of the Master seems to have been lost. Service to others, whether civil or ministerial, too frequently masks the secret ambitions and the inordinate lust for power and control over others.

I have to ask myself over and over again whether I am sincere in my willingness to help and to care for others. Or could it be that, in all honesty, I am actually using, exploiting and manipulating others for my own selfish ends?

"Anyone who wants to become great among you must be your servant. Anyone who wants to become first among you must be a slave to all. For the Son of Man himself did not come to be served but to serve, and to give his life as a ransom for many." (Mk. 10:44-45)

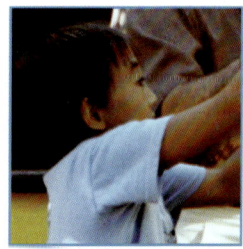

I love you...no strings attached.

Beware the Gift with a Hook

"A gift is not a gift if you know the giver." (Anon)

When fishing I bring along some fat, wriggly worms or other tempting morsels to bait my hidden hook. To a hungry whopper lurking in the weeds below (that's how a dedicated fisherman fantasizes), the dangling lure is too much to resist and bam!—one slurp later, the fish is hooked. The "gift" I offered was a barbed hook wearing worm clothing.

I get similar baited hooks offered to me all the time. Just this morning I received my 99th begging letter, soliciting anything from $5 to $500 or more—although "the $35 amount would really help." This particular "personalized letter," sent bulk mail, didn't include free, self-stick name and address labels—of which I now have about 5,000—but there were some tacky greeting cards that stirred a bit of guilt in me to remit something.

This latest appeal unveiled a clever new gimmick. Along with a list of specific amounts of money that would "serve 13, 16 or 29 hungry persons," vouchers bearing my name as the actual donor were included. I was invited to return the vouchers with my donation. So as the hungry persons dined, they would see my very own name as the kind stranger who paid for their meal. Broken down, the meal would cost a mere $1.62—about the price of a hamburger and a cola. Big deal.

There was even a reminder that each donation was tax deductible.

What was the uneasy, negative reaction that welled up inside of me? Would this donation be in fact a form of selfishness disguised as generosity? Why was it necessary that the hungry diner know my name? And that tax write-off. Even if it fits the IRS's definition of charity, is it a genuine act of generosity or am I merely feathering my own nest? To be perfectly clear, I think it is proper to avail myself of any tax break offered to me. But love and kindness are not defined by legal terms, and on honest analysis, am I truly giving a gift—making a sacrifice—or is it only a mask for charity to gain something for myself?

Put simply, love means to give something of myself to meet the needs of another. When I am so often tempted to use someone's misfortune to my advantage and gain, do I fall for it? I am the one and only person who knows the truth of it.

· · · · · · · · ·

Jesus once came into a town where he met a leprous man. Religious law forbade a leper or any diseased person, legally unclean, to have any contact with healthy persons. After all, the widespread belief and conviction was that the disease was an incurable affliction brought on by God's vengeance for sin, and therefore well-deserved. Symbolically, the leper was a soul condemned to hell, beyond redemption, guilty of unforgivable sin.

In this New Testament telling, however, it was the leper's deep conviction about this man Jesus that urged him to ignore the prohibition.

 Collapsing on his knees in front of Jesus, he bowed low to the ground and pleaded, "Sir, if you want to, you can make me well." (Lk 5:12-14)

To prompt reflection, I often describe Jesus recoiling in disgust, citing the law, and berating the leper for his brazen audacity: "Get away! How dare you! Don't you know the law?! You're unclean because of your sins and yet you have the nerve to get close to me? Get away, you repulsive thing, or I'll report you to the authorities and have you punished."

Preposterous? Why so? If Jesus did not gag at the sight of the pus and the stench of putrid flesh, if he wasn't forced to suppress an urge to retch, a natural and spontaneous reaction in the face of such ugliness, then the telling of this entire incident would be meaningless.

Jesus had to feel the same natural reactions as I would to anything so repellent or unsavory, since he was fully human. Being human, he was like me in all things, except he did not sin—which is to say, he never deliberately hurt a fellow human being.

In fact, like Jesus I also am capable of great virtue and heroism by sheer determination and self-conquest. I have the potential of performing the mightiest acts by sheer grit, guts and grace. St. Francis of Assisi began his conversion by cleansing and dressing the wasted limbs of lepers. I have experienced and seen the loving ministrations of my mother, of nurses and doctors, of my own religious brothers and sisters and others who refused to turn away from similar revolting situations.

I picture how Jesus summoned up his inner reserves, praying to do his Father's will, possibly swallowing hard and even holding his breath, lest he gag, reaching down and lifting the poor wretch quivering at his feet. I even imagine Jesus pulling him up and toward himself, stroking and comforting him tenderly and whispering into his ear—this lonely soul who had been shunned and despised for so many long years—"Of course I want to, you poor thing, be cured!"

In an instant, the hideous disease vanished. The gaping, suppurating holes in his flesh closed, his fingers and toes were replaced; his skin was baby-smooth again. His bursting heart could not be contained. He was jumping and dancing from sheer joy, shouting, "You did it! You did it! You healed me! How can I ever thank you? I can't wait to see my family again!"

Then followed a puzzling sequel. Smiling in satisfaction, Jesus waited for the healed leper's excitement to subside. Then very oddly he ordered him to keep his cure a secret and to tell no one about it. Tell no one?! Why not? The healed man could hardly wait to rejoin his alienated family whom he hadn't seen for years. He couldn't wait to tell them what this wonderful man had done for him. Now this same man was telling him not to share the good news.

If I had been the healer I'd be tempted to strut about smugly, proudly parading the healed leper around like a sideshow oddity. I might even consider sending him a whopping bill. After all, isn't that what most caregivers do for services rendered?

But not Jesus. His whole focus had been on the newly healed man who was overcome with joy. "Are you happy?" The smiling Jesus asked gently. "Am I happy?! Am I happy?! I can't tell you how happy I am," the man kept exclaiming.

"Good. So am I," Jesus said, smiling some more. "I did it for you. So let's keep it between us, and don't tell anyone who did it, all right?"

· · · · · · · · ·

The lesson here is a simple one: Be careful not to parade your good deeds before others to attract notice; if you do this you will lose all reward from your heavenly Father. When you give alms, don't trumpet it. This is what hypocrites do to win people's admiration, so that's all the credit they'll receive. When you give alms, your left hand must not know what your right is doing. Your gift-giving must be secret. Then your Father who sees all that is done in secret will reward you. (Mt 6:1-4)

I always think of this advice from Jesus when I see bronze plaques on church walls and public buildings, and lists of donors and benefactors in programs, complete even with dollar amounts. Is this any different from the large ads of commercial and professional firms? The gift is no longer a gift, it is an advertisement.

Closer to what Jesus suggests are those posted as a gift from an "anonymous donor." It's like God, the Secret Lover who never takes credit for the blessings which fill our lives… after all, this reflection has been about love, hasn't it?

"*Look at the flowers...*"

Saying it with Flowers

"Look at the flowers," Jesus said (Lk 12:27)

"Here, take these to school," my mother said, handing me and my sisters large bundles of spicy-scented roses wrapped in cones of newspaper. We were third-and fourth-graders off to school, laden with these sweet gifts for our teachers. And Sister Jamesine, whom I adored, would reach for the bundle, bury her delicate nose into the blooms and, with an appreciative squeeze for me - the part I liked - gush her grateful pleasure.

It was a nice way to start the day. When I recall these childhood experiences I am forced to consider what possible reason Mom might have had in sending me to school with this substitute of an apple for the teacher. Did she think I needed to win Sister's favor to maintain my academic status with a sweet-smelling bribe?

As I reflect on her entire life, Mom was a giver, ever thoughtful and generous. Not only gifts of flowers but of cakes, cookies, embroideries and, in fact, whole Chinese dinners. She delighted in surprising others with taste treats, which won her the title of "World's Best Cook."

But it was her magnificent obsession with flowers that set her apart. In spite of the fierce Arizona heat, she managed to fill our half-acre with every kind of vegetable and fruit tree, along with large plots of hot orange and yellow zinnias and marigolds, spicy stocks, perky snapdragons, rosette portulacas, elegant tuberoses, bright-eyed daisies - all embedded in fluffy, bouncy alyssum. These images are indelibly fixed in my memory today, even as I plant the cousins of all these flowers in my own garden.

It was the five-plot rose garden, however, in the grass center of our oval-shaped driveway that was mom's real pride. I can still picture the dozen bushes in each plot, which yielded the glorious, prize-winning blooms which we bundled off to school.

All the flowers of all the years are long gone. And yet the memory of them and their effect linger like a long-lasting heavenly fragrance.

· · · · · · · · ·

The loveliness of flowers in my life is a constant reminder of God's marvelous creativity and never-ending thoughtfulness and care. Blossoms show me that with each "ohhh" and "ahhh" I breathe, God the unseen Creator is somewhere in the wings, smiling at my pleasure. And that must apply even to those who are unaware that there is a God at all or who blindly deny he exists. How can anyone think that beauty such as this just happened by chance?

A world without flowers would be empty of their delicious perfume, wondrous rainbow hues and perfect shapes, and our eager, springtime anticipation of their arrival in tight buds. How empty the world would be without the delicate, heady aroma of peach and cherry, almond and plum, orange and apple blossoms that foretell the coming harvest of juice-laden fruit of every kind. Neither would there be the mouth-watering, nutritious gold of honey gathered by tireless, busy bees.

Lovers would have to express in their own bumbling words their affection for one another without an armful of crimson roses. As children, my siblings and I would have gone to school and ground away at our books without the benefit of the color and fragrance that filled the classroom from the bouquets we brought, courtesy of Mom.

Love is the reason behind anything I do to bring pleasure and happiness into someone's life. Everything that God has done and, moment by moment, continues to do in my life, is for my enjoyment and good. It is love in action. How do I know? Because God is Love. (1 Jn 4:8)

The use of the word "love" here is not a verb as in "God loves." That could imply that God might act for reasons other than love and even stop loving at some point. Rather, love is the very definition or synonym of God, God's other name. Love is God's very essence. This means that it is impossible for God to stop loving or to do the opposite, that is, to hurt or despise or destroy.

This truth is why Paul assured the Ephesians, "God loved us with so much love he was generous with his mercy. When we were dead through our sins, he did not condemn us. He brought us to life with Christ. It is through grace (God's free gift of love) we have been given a place with him in heaven... We are God's work of art, created in Jesus Christ to live the good life, as from the beginning he has meant us to live it." (Eph.2:4-10)

Now it's clearer to me why gardenias are so intoxicating, why orchid leis welcome the stranger with fragrance, and garlands of tiny roses crown lovely brides. "Have you noticed the flowers?" God seems to be asking. "Have you smelled the perfume? I did it for you. If you like it, I'm glad."

No doubt Jesus was thinking of how enthralled we would be when he urged, "Look at the flowers - the lilies and poppies which carpet the Galilean hills in springtime - look at them closely, be amazed at their exquisite coloring, drink in their heady fragrance, touch and feel their unmatchable texture - here today and gone tomorrow." (Lk 12:27)

It seems so extravagant, yet he goes on to explain, "If your Father lavishes such tender care on these gorgeous short-lived little creations, how do you think he will care for you? You are worth so much more than the lovely flowers. Can't you see how precious you are to him?" (Lk 12:24 passim)

Now it can be told: FTD Florists cribbed from the Scriptures when they coined the slogan: "Say It With Flowers." After all, with each flower God is saying, "I love you."

The loveliest thing about a woman is that she is a person - shadowed often in tantalizing mystery.

Woman,
 You are mystery.

What is seen at quarter phase is spring moon lovely.

What must be your beauty when the moon is full?

The Big Difference

Professor Higgins of *My Fair Lady* fame laments in frustration over the maddening behavior and perplexing antics of his protégé, Eliza Doolittle, who has stolen his heart, "Oh, why can't a woman be more like a man?"

His question hangs like ripe fruit on a tree just beyond reach. It's a problem that has proven to be an insoluble, infuriating riddle to the male of the human species since the beginning of time. Eastern mythology, however, offers a plausible account of the origin of the problem. Here it is as best as I can recall from having heard it told once long ago:

In the beginning, after God had formed Adam and breathed life into his clay form, he turned to the next task of creating a partner to be a helpmate. But lo! God discovered that he had unwittingly used up his supply of solid and durable materials in creating Adam.

In this predicament, after much deep thought, in his wisdom, God decided to do the next best thing. He gathered from Nature what had not been used in creating Adam and did as follows: he took the song of a meadowlark, the scent of jasmine, the curl of an ocean wave, the curve of an elephant's trunk, the delicate lace of roses, the grace of running deer, the cooing of doves, the clinging of tendrils, the industry of bees and the affection of lovebirds.

To these elements God added the fierceness of tigers and the purring of kittens, the cawing of crows and chattering of jays (flocks of them, I'd imagine), the tears of storm clouds and the musical wind through the trees, the fickleness of fawns and the hardness of flint, the pride of peacocks and the tenacity of hounds, the cold of frost and the warmth of burning coals.

Combining all of these elements God created Eve, the woman, and brought her to Adam. On beholding her, Adam was elated and joyously took her to himself.

By month's end, Adam was back begging to talk to God. He was angry and very frustrated. Bitterly he complained; "I can't explain it, God, but this woman causes me more pain than pleasure. Please, take her back." And God said: "Very well."

A short week passed. Adam again approached God, this time sheepish and contrite. "God," said Adam, "I am ashamed. Ever since I returned that woman to you, life has been miserable. I am lonely. I miss her smile, and her laugh was like the ringing of bells. I remember how we played and danced together. She was soft and delicious to hold and caress, and her tender kisses were like sweet wine. Please, give her back to me?"

"By all means, take her," God said. (I can't hack it with her any longer, either)." So Adam joyfully embraced the woman Eve and took her to his home like a found treasure.

Incredibly, after only another week, Adam was back, full of shame and apologetic. "God," he cried, "I don't know how it is, but this woman is driving me mad. She constantly disagrees with me; she chatters incessantly; she cries over nothing; she nags me constantly and never stops finding fault with me. Please, take her back."

By now God was weary of Adam's complaining and whining. He would have no more of it. "Enough!" God snapped. "Away with you! Go work it out the best you can,"

"But I can't live with her!" Adam groaned.

"Neither can you live without her," God retorted. With that, God turned away from Adam and returned to His task of caring for the rest of the universe.

So there you are, Professor Higgins. Simply put, Eliza Doolittle is different, period. But rather than complaining about it and trying to alter her, you must try to adjust to it and see why it's possible to cheer the difference. Like two faces of a coin, a woman supplies what is lacking in the male, while, on the other hand, a man provides what a woman longs for and truly needs.

Historically and culturally, women have been subjected to unbelievable abuse and oppression. Men have sometimes treated women cruelly, depriving them of equality and opportunity to develop their potential. Rather than being treated with respect, women have been stripped of their dignity and treated as pleasure objects, degraded, exploited and then discarded.

Meantime, our world has been dominated by male machismo and bluffing (Knock-the-chip-off-my-shoulder kind of dares). As a result, untold billions have been spent on the most obscene weapons and countless millions of young lives have been cut short in wars declared by arrogant leaders. The beautiful world has been ravaged by continual violence and exploitation. Whole cities have been obliterated. Entire generations of vibrant lives have been exterminated and families shattered. To what gain? What would happen, I wonder, if women were given a major role in the governing of people and nations?

Beyond women's external attractiveness lie warm hearts and an innate empathy with the well-being and pain of others. Their maternal instincts of nurturing and protecting would prevail. Their natural God-like qualities of patience, mercy and compassion would flower.

What men seem to lack is the warmth and tenderness so characteristic of women nurses comforting at a bedside or a mother's gentle soothing away the tears of a child who scraped a knee. I have witnessed with awe and admiration the 24-hour acts of a mother feeding, washing and clothing her brood. And predators, beast or human, beware the fury of a mother protecting her child with no concern for her own safety!

A woman friend had backed me to the wall and lectured me about the neglected qualities of woman in history and human affairs, much to humanity's great loss. Her argument can't be ignored, as one can see.

If women had a larger share of authority, she declared, wars would be rarities. Hunger and homelessness would be largely footnotes in history. If women decided where to channel public funds, the scandalous blight of our decayed, smelly and trashy urban areas would be swept clean. Women can't stand dirt.

Simplistic? Unrealistic? Then consider the enormous achievements of a few religious women who establish and operate huge hospitals, schools and refuges for orphans, runaways and prostitutes. With unshakable faith, these faith-filled women work fearlessly with the skill and courage of the highest-paid corporate executives.

At any rate, the sad world condition, so torn by hatred, suspicion and carnage, is evidence that men have squandered their opportunities. It's time to give women the chance to exercise their innate wisdom, talents and instincts, so long ignored or suppressed.

I saw a sign on a wall with a witty twist to the bible story of the Three Wise Men from the east who sought out the newborn King and Savior. It read:

Three Wise Women would have:

Asked directions; Arrived on time;

Helped deliver the baby; Cleaned the stable;

Made a casserole; Brought practical gifts: diapers & toys

—and there would be peace on earth.

Any male want to challenge that?

*I choose you, my Love, for who you are
and who you may become;
To assist you in youur tasks;
To give of myself to the fullest development of your life;
To be challenged by you to the fullest development of my own life;
To trust you in all ways and to be faithful to you in all things.
I will love you and comfort you.
I will honor you and keep you
In sickness and in health, in good times and in bad.
I will ennoble you always – respecting your freedom to be who you are
and to share in responsible service to the world
of which we both remain a part.*

Covenant

"Do You Give Yourself to This Man/Woman?"

"As the Father has loved me, so have I loved you. Live on in my love. I tell you this that my joy may be yours and your joy may be complete. My commandment is: Love one another as I have loved you. There is no greater love that this: to lay your life down for your friend," Jesus taught. (Jn 15:9-14)

I was reading from John's Gospel as food for thought at a Bangkok wedding between a lovely Thai bride and a handsome Filipino groom. They had met and fallen in love while enrolled at Columbia University in New York.

My presence as a Catholic priest was to represent his faith, and I came as a lucky guest of his family. On her side, the family had engaged the ministry of a Buddhist monk, as over 90% of the population in Thailand practices Buddhism.

I reflected on Jesus' words before this mostly non-Christian gathering. "To love is the opposite of taking; it is to give of oneself for the happiness and the good of the one you love. The gorgeous lilies and orange blossoms that make up your bridal bouquet, for example, are actually dying. They have been cut to help make this wedding your dream-come-true by contributing their exquisite beauty and fragrance.

"In the same way," I went on, "at last night's pre-nuptial banquet your mother pointed to a platter on our table and commented, 'Just think. That fish was alive and swimming in a tank only an hour ago'."

"And there it lay, a large, whole succulent bass, steamed in its own juices, soy sauce and sesame oil and sprinkled with finely chopped green onions, ginger and cilantro." (As far as I am concerned, this Asian method of preparing and serving fish is the best lip-smacking style of eating seafood.)

I could sense that the congregants were puzzled by this prosaic and even crass reference during a wedding ceremony to eating fish. I even rubbed my belly and rolled my eyes as I described how the fish had been completely devoured and was at that moment nourishing our bodies.

"That fish," I continued, "died for us. It made our banquet sumptuous by giving up its life for us. But it didn't do so by choice. It had to be killed for our good pleasure. Now that is the underlying principle of life: Everything is created to serve the needs of something else."

"The big difference is that, whereas the fish fought and struggled to stay alive, it was put to death nonetheless. But when we speak of humans laying down their lives for someone else, it is a deliberate decision and choice to do so. That is love."

"Now when you say you are getting married, you are declaring to each other and to the whole world that you are unselfishly giving yourself to your beloved. In essence then you are not getting a wife, you are giving yourself to this woman. You are not getting a husband; you are giving yourself to this man. Is that clear? Now that you know what you're getting into, do you still want to go through with it? If so, then we may proceed…"

After the wedding two strapping young Thai men approached. "Very interesting talk, sir. But as you know, we are Buddhists, and we do not kill. Live and let live is our teaching."

"You mean you don't eat fish? You don't eat meat?" I asked, curious and incredulous. "Oh, we eat fish, we eat meat," they were clear about that.

"Well, where do you get it?" I asked

"Interesting question…" they said as they walked away pondering. Later I was informed that butchers in Thailand are either Christian or Moslems.

Covenant: *I take you* vs. *I give you myself*

Lucie and Gordon are my special Jewish/Catholic couple at whose marriage I officiated years ago. The following format, with some slight modification, is essentially theirs. I've used it for marriages ever since. Invariably the ceremony evokes the most enthusiastic reactions such as: "How moving! That was the most beautiful, meaningful, inspiring wedding I've ever witnessed, etc., etc." Here it follows, along with some ad lib comments I sometimes make, careful not to destroy the gravity of the occasion. To begin with, the couple are directed to face and look into each other's eyes, where one may hope to read honesty and sincerity.

A DECLARATION OF INTENT Lucie and Gordon, do you freely choose (out of limitless possibilities) one another to be husband and wife, to live together within the covenant of marriage (covenant being your word and promise made in good faith)? Will you love one another - by comforting one another, honoring and keeping one another - in sickness and in health, in good times and in bad times? Will you always strive to ennoble each other, always respecting the other's freedom, dignity and individuality to grow and to be of service to the world? If so, we may proceed... Now as a symbol of what you hold in your hearts, please join your hands. Bear in mind that if your intentions do not match your words, then nothing happens. It would be only a charade.

CONSENT AND COMMITMENT (Each in turn.) "I freely choose you for who you are and who you may become (even if you run off with someone else?) — to assist you in your tasks — to be sensitive to your needs — to give of myself to the fullest development of your life — to be challenged by you to the fullest development of my own life (so as to be able to love you with even greater intensity) — to trust you in all ways — and to be faithful to you in all things. (The mutual promise is sealed with a kiss.)

Once Gordon has made his commitment, he's reminded that, as of this moment, he has willingly surrendered himself totally to Lucie, to devote his lifelong energies to her good and happiness. He does so without any conditions or proviso such as: "provided she commits herself to me as well." His total, unilateral commitment is in that sense an enormous risk, an act of total trust.

Next, Lucie is asked if she would like to reciprocate. She does so and then repeats the identical promise of total commitment. This mutual gift of one to the other is 100% — 100%, not 50% — 50%. The challenge and task that face them for the duration of their lives is to be true to their original fervor. Should either or both begin to renege, to cheat and to compromise, the perfect balance with which they have begun will start to wobble and twist, torturing the framework of the original promise. Eventually, the marriage will disintegrate and crash in flames of distrust and even hatred.

If Lucie and Gordon live up to their original promises faithfully, they will most surely find joy and fulfillment in each other all through their lives, and no power on earth can ever take it away from them.

What Love and Marriage Mean

COMMENTARY

"Everything is created to serve the needs of something else." I have seen bumper stickers proclaiming that "Meat is Dead, Ugh!", implying that eating meat is repugnant and, by association, so is the butchering of animals for food. I find that kind of thinking sentimental and specious. Other living things, such as onions and lettuce, cabbage, carrots and radishes -- all vegetables -- are living and doing quite well in the ground until they are pulled up and harvested! And there's nothing like a delicious, crisp salad. Enjoy!

"I freely choose you for who you are and who you may become—even if you run off with someone else." This is the astounding implication of unconditional love. Love has no reason nor logic. Love simply is. I do not love because of anything. I simply love or I don't. For better or for worse. In good times and in bad times. Therefore if I can truly say, "'I'll always love you, no matter what" to my beloved who has broken my heart by betraying me, then I would be speaking like God. The love of God for each of His children is absolute and without condition. There are no ifs, ands or buts to God's love. St. Paul makes no bones about it: "Nothing that exists, nothing still to come, not any power, nor any created thing, can ever come between us and the love of God made visible in Christ Jesus." (Rom. 8:38). "God loved us with so much love that He was generous with His mercy: when we were dead through our sins, He rescued us, brought us to life and has given us a place with Him in heaven in Christ." (Eph. 2:4.)

WHY DO PEOPLE MARRY, ANYWAY? The answer is self-evident, isn't it? People marry because they love each other. How naive. For many, if not most would-be marriages, I have found that love is not the reason at all. As a result, I think that because love is absent, there is no marriage. Therefore the eventual breakup isn't really a divorce and divorce statistics should be revised.

I have long concluded that marriages are too often entered into for a whole list of reasons other than love, such as: searching for companionship and security, money and status, sex and maybe, children; even, believe it or not, to become a citizen or to escape shame by legitimizing a child conceived out of wedlock.

If marriage is the commitment of love between two persons, and it is, then any union entered into for a lesser intention is a faux marriage, as phony as a three-dollar bill. So those multiple so-called marriages (five, six, seven times?!), so notorious among celebrities, become mere temporary cohabitation under the lovely and sublime guise of marriage. It is gross mockery of the most noble relationship possible between two human beings.

How many bright-eyed brides fantasize about their Galahads and Prince Charmings who will come and sweep them off their feet and cuddle them forever! And how many

Galahads and Prince Charmings dream of their gorgeous princesses to bed down and to parade around like some hard-won trophy? Marriage becomes an approved and florid way of getting something for oneself.

Think of the energy and money expended on ritual and ceremonies that surround a wedding: announcements and invitations, showers and receptions, travel and reservations, limousines and hotels, florists and photographers (and now videographers), bakers and chefs, gowns and tuxedos, the use of a church and reception hall, and O yes, perhaps a stipend for the clergyman.

And too often, sometimes not too long after, the happy union goes up in smoke. Why? Because there never was a fundamental intention and desire to let go of one's inherent selfishness. The basic notion of commitment is for the happiness and good of the beloved, not for oneself. Until and unless this gift of self-giving is made, the union sits on a precarious foundation. And as long as one or both persons lack this essential motive, it's only a matter of time until the shorted nature of the relationship rears its ugly, selfish head and destroys what began so lavishly.

Do This In Memory of Me

These are the words of Jesus which form the heart and focal point of every Catholic Mass. They follow on the heels of his loving commitment to each and every person: "This is My Body which is given up and broken FOR you; this is My Blood poured out FOR you and FOR all people without exception to cancel out your sins and indebtedness." Think of the immensity of his love for all his sisters and brothers in the human family!

So whenever I do anything FOR someone, such as to heal, to comfort, to pardon, to bring happiness, it is saying, "I love you." No wonder communicants celebrating the Eucharist lift their voices in grateful, joyous acknowledgment: "Lord, by your cross and resurrection, you have set us free. You are the Savior of the world!"

The aged old man, Simeon, held Mary's child and said in prayer,

"Now, Master, you may dismiss your servant in peace. For my eyes have seen your salvation which you prepared for all nations to see..."
Lk 2:29

New Cloth and a New Wineskin

I was once privileged to address a distinguished gathering of attorneys, judges and state legislators at an annual Red Mass, so-called in honor of the martyred Sir St. Thomas More, their patron saint.

I was doubly grateful that it was the memory of my late brother, Judge Thomas Tang, being honored on this occasion. He had been a judge of the U.S. Ninth Circuit Court of Appeals, and this would be the ideal opportunity to face some serious issues in the name of the court's patron saint.

I prefaced my remarks with a caveat (good legal term): "This is not going to be your usual ten-minute homily. Rather, it will be more the length of a legal brief, so you should all settle back comfortably and resign yourselves."

I began with the dramatic gospel scene in John, Chapter 8, of a woman caught in *flagrante delicto*—adultery. For such a crime the law prescribed that she be stoned to death. Jesus is put on the horns of a dilemma: observe the law or show mercy? The bloodthirsty mob press and taunt him to make a decision. If he pardons her, it would be grounds for his own conviction. Jesus merely squats casually and doodles on the ground, driving the mob to a frenzy. At last, standing tall and glowering into the circle of hate-filled faces, he throws down the gauntlet: "Whoever has never sinned, be the first to throw a stone. I dare you."

Ever so slowly they begin to skulk away, starting with the eldest. Finally, only Jesus and the woman remain. "Isn't there anyone left to condemn you?" Jesus asks.

"There's no one," she replies meekly.

"Well, then I don't condemn you, either," Jesus says, dismissing her and urging her to change her ways.

What's going on here? Why didn't Christ condemn her when she was clearly guilty? I answered my own question with a personal experience. While director of Serra Retreat House in Malibu in the early '80s, I was summoned to jury duty.

It was a sabbatical year, and I relished the chance to experience jury service. I even dressed in mufti lest my clerical clothes provide a reason to disqualify me. Sure enough, a nun in habit was summarily dismissed, as was a UCLA professor, causing me to wonder why such highly qualified and dependable candidates were rejected.

Suddenly the bailiff called out "Reverend Emery Tang." He had blown my cover! I approached the bench in my plain clothes. The Chinese judge was quizzical, "He called you Reverend, sir. What kind of Reverend are you?"

In a moment of levity I might have answered, "Very,' your honor" but felt it more prudent to say, "I'm the Franciscan priest director at Serra Retreat in Malibu."

"Oh, yes, now I recall," the judge acknowledged and went on, "Well, why aren't you in uniform?"

"I didn't want my collar and garb to prevent me from serving on a jury, sir," I explained.

The trial involved two youths accused of assault and rape. The prosecutor was actually a Catholic retreatant serving as a deputy D.A. who knew me and, oddly, did not object to my presence.

One defense attorney probed, "Does anyone in your family belong to law enforcement?" "No," I said, "but I do have a brother who is a judge."

"Will that hinder you from making an objective judgment in this case?" he asked.

"Oh I doubt it."

"Why not? Please explain yourself," he pressed

"Well, first of all, my brother and I rarely talk about each other's professional work. But, as I understand it, his task as a judge is not to make laws but to determine whether, in a given case, an accused has violated an established law. If so, to what degree, and then to apply a sanction which he judges fitting. Whereas, in my role as a priest, I think my task is to get people off the hook."

At this, the defense attorney instantly turned to the judge and said, "Your honor, we'll take him!"

To satisfy your curiosity, we the jury did in fact convict the pair, based on incriminating evidence not reasonably explained away—and the judge concurred.

But back to my description of a priest's role, that is, "to get people off the hook." Every Catholic makes a confession with the presumption that he will receive absolution or forgiveness of sins, no matter how heinous. In fact, there are even those who, if refused absolution by an intransigent priest, will choose never to set foot in a Catholic church again.

Guilty as the adulterous woman was, Jesus defiantly exonerated her at the risk of his life.

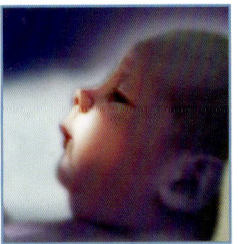

"I love you so much."
-Abba

"The Earlier Law is abolished and is replaced by something better – a new covenant with the hope that brings us nearer to God." (Heb 7:18-19)

And Now for The Truth...
Until Now It has Been B.C.–
From Now on It Is A.D.

"No one puts a piece of unshrunken cloth onto an old cloak, because the patch pulls away from the cloak and the tear gets worse." (Mt 9:16)

In the Scriptures there's a story about a lawyer who was trying to trip Jesus up. He asked, "Master, what must I do to inherit eternal life?"

Jesus said, "What is written in the Law? What do you read there?"

The lawyer replied, "You must love the Lord your God with all your heart, soul, mind and strength - and your neighbor as yourself."

"That's right," Jesus said. "Do this and you will live." (Lk 10:25)

The term "law" is used equivocally here. The lawyer was a scholar versed in the 613 legal prescriptions in the Torah, considered to have been revealed and promulgated by God himself. They were divided into 248 positive and 365 prohibitive prescriptions of the law, each binding with equal force. To violate any of them brought down divine punishment in the form of personal and national retribution. The lawyer was suggesting that one specific law ranked above all others.

Jesus affirms that there is but one central law governing all reality and human behavior

"On this principle of love rest the Law (Torah) and the prophets" (Mt 22:40) This is the Law of Love. It is not a juridical law, such as attorneys deal with. Rather, it is the law of my very nature, the intrinsic law of my being.

Love is God or God is Love. Love is God's other name. I have been made out of love by God, in order to love and be loved. Hence I am made in the image of God. This is the ultimate truth governing all reality. Thus, all of creation is a manifestation of the love of God and is designed for the pleasure and happiness of all people. This universal, fundamental law of love is immutable and absolute.

To love means I freely choose to do only what is good for myself or someone else. It brings with it happiness. Love fulfills the purpose of my being. The power and beauty of love lie in its pure gratuity and total voluntary nature. It is freely bestowed. It cannot be coerced or legislated. And while love is the most challenging of all motives, it is also the most rewarding.

Freedom, however, is a door that swings in two directions. As a human, I am often driven by arrogance and pride, anger, jealousy, greed and other forms of selfishness, and will often choose to harm and make myself or someone else miserable. I can actually choose to be a criminal or, in a religious context, a sinner. In so doing I become an enemy who inflicts pain and destroys happiness. Am I not sometimes my own worst enemy?

When I have been injured unjustly, my tendency is to strike back and to inflict commensurate pain and suffering. In which case I become as evil as the one who first hurt me. This retaliatory reaction was actually sanctioned in the Old Testament as the Law of Talion: "An eye for an eye; a tooth for a tooth. "(Levit. 24:20) Even God was portrayed as an avenger: "Vengeance is mine," says the Lord. (Heb. 10:30)

With his coming into our world, Jesus initiated the Christian era, marked as A.D. (Anno Domini–in the Year or Era of the Lord), now entering its third millennium. Jesus' role and mission was not as a legislator, even as he abrogated the Talion of the Old Testament and instituted a New Covenant between God and us his people, and between us and all other people: "Until now you have heard it said, 'An eye for an eye, a tooth for a tooth.' From now on I say, 'Love one another, yes, but love your enemy as well!'" (Mt. 5:38-44 passim)

This was not a new law. Jesus was revealing the magnificent truth: that God is and has always been the loving Abba (papa), and every person is his child, a precious son or a daughter, created to share in his divine nature of goodness, love, peace and compassion.

Jesus points out how foolish it is to put new wine into an old wineskin, since it will swell, burst and spill the good wine. Or, using another domestic example, he showed how it is a waste of time to sew a new cloth piece onto a shrunken old rag, since it will shrink and tear away. By this he is describing how the rigid demands of justice in the Old Testament are incompatible with the mercy and compassion of his gospel's New Covenant. You can't have it both ways. Put quite plainly, you can't hang a person with love.

Jesus goes on: "Do good to those who hate you, bless those who curse you. Pray for those who treat you badly. If someone slaps you, offer the other cheek. If someone takes your shirt from you"- instead of suing the hell out of him -"offer him your coat, too. If you love only those who love you, what thanks can you expect? Instead, love your enemies and do good; lend without any hope of return.

You will have a great reward and be like children of the Most High God, for he himself is kind to the ungrateful and the wicked. Do not judge and you will not be; grant pardon and you will be pardoned as well. Give, and there will be gifts for you."
(Lk 6:27-35 passim)

Jesus is the Way and the Truth. There is no other. To ignore, circumvent or substitute something other than his example and teaching, as humans have done for two millennia, is to invite sure disappointment and ultimate ruin.

I am aware that these moral concepts are completely and painfully alien to the justice system, and as a citizen with feet planted in both the secular and religious worlds, I cannot find balance in my thinking and peace in my heart. I am alternately compassionate and vindictive in my attitudes and behavior.

So what can I do? Is society ready for and even capable of a radical overhaul of the entire justice system of the country? Is it possible to reeducate and convert an entire citizenry to the values of Jesus' gospel?

It's no secret about the growing skepticism and cynicism over courts, judges, lawyers and the jury system. My brother Judge Tom once asked a group over dinner, "What do you do when you find a lawyer up to his neck in sand?" We didn't know, so he gave us the answer, "You go get more sand."

I wonder if it's time to examine the value and the consequences of the "innocent until proven guilty" principle. After all, if in fact I have committed a crime or sinned against someone, I am not innocent. It's like the culprit standing before the presiding judge who asked, "Are you innocent or guilty?" The culprit muttered, "Isn't that what we came here to find out, your honor?"

And then the cat and mouse game begins. Tons of money, mountains of briefs and hours and hours of labor later, followed by a solemn declaration of innocent or guilty, does not guarantee that, in fact, the accused is innocent or guilty.

In one of our country's most enduring legends, when George Washington cut down the cherry tree, he couldn't tell a lie and deny it, so he admitted the truth. What was the consequence? He was made first president of the United States. Whatever happened to honesty, integrity and accepting of responsibility? Wasn't I reared with the notion that, if I have been responsible for some wrongdoing, I should own up to it? Isn't this the first requisite in Alcoholics Anonymous and other addiction programs before rehabilitation is possible? The denial of truth and reality is the root cause of dysfunction in all human relationships.

In today's justice system, the last thing one ever does is to admit to the truth. Even we religious are instructed by our insurance carriers never to admit to responsibility in an accident. Honest Abe Lincoln, another president, declared, "I do the best I know how - the very best I can, and I mean to keep doing so until the end. If the end brings me out all right, what is said against me won't amount to anything. If the end brings me out wrong, ten angels swearing I was right won't make a difference."

Which brings me back to the priest who defines himself as one who gets people off the hook. The requirement is that the offender comes and admits his or her wrong and asks for pardon, which in the name of an all-compassionate God, is never refused. So maybe that part of the Fifth Amendment ought to be re-amended: "No person shall be compelled to be witness against himself."

Judge Tang risked his career and experienced rude and vicious calumny when he tried to meld the two great contraries: the letter of the law and understanding compassion. In his practice he strove to preserve the notion that laws are made for the good of the people, not people for the good of laws. It was a difficult and challenging task.

If violators and offenders of the law were assured that they would always be treated with understanding and fairness, that consequences incurred would not be retaliatory measures but means of correction and rehabilitation, that pardon and forgiveness were actually possible, many more crimes would be solved without the tedium of endless cat and mouse trials. Is it only a pipe dream to consider this approach to human weakness and perversity a possibility as the world moves forward into the third Millennium? For the last two thousand years we have tried everything but the way Jesus showed us to live at peace with one another. Isn't it time society finally learned?

When we least expect it, Hope bursts through our clouds of desolation.
Look for that surprise.

An act of love in Genoa, Italy.

"If you want to," said the leper to Jesus, "you can cure me."
(Lk 5:13)

Passing the Jewel

A weary traveler once encountered an elderly bearded monk trudging along the same mountain road. As he drew up next to the old man he greeted him and was about to pass. The monk motioned to him to pause and rest awhile underneath a tree to share a drink. As the monk opened his knapsack the traveler spotted a glittering jewel inside. "My, what is that beautiful gem?" he exclaimed. Without hesitating, the old man placed it in his hand for closer examination. Its colors flashed and sparkled like a thousand diamonds, dazzling the traveler. "What must it be worth?!" he gaped and wondered, fingering it gently.

"If you want to have it, take it," the old monk said simply. Eyes bugged, hardly believing his ears, the traveler closed his fist over the stone, stammered some clumsy thanks and walked away, slowly at first, then broke into a run as fast as his legs could move. What he clutched in his fist was worth a king's ransom! He would be able to buy anything he ever wanted. What luck!

Weeks passed into months as the traveler fingered the jewel in his pocket every day. Then one day he decided to do a very strange thing. He retraced his steps to locate the old monk. He found him very near the same place where he had first met him. He placed the gem in the old man's hand.

"Old man," he said, "I have treasured your gift every day I have had it. Now you can have it back. But there is something else I would like to have. I want that *spirit* that prompted you to give me the precious jewel in the first place."

-Homily Helps-

What was the spirit behind the old monk's gift? What was his motive? What did he stand to gain from his action? Why would he give the jewel to a total stranger?

The monk's generosity was a pure gift. He asked for nothing in return. He knew it would thrill the stranger, as it surely did.

The monk's action can only be Love. Love does wild and crazy things that don't make sense. Love is profligate, lavishly scattering good things in its path. Love doesn't count the cost. There is no logic to Love, no why to it. It just is.

Love is the force that fills and binds the universe into one marvelous, harmonious whole. Love is the life energy in all living things. Love is the boundless source of the design and beauty in creation.

How did Love ever start? Where did it come from? I can't even begin to guess the answer to these questions. So, like a student in an exam, I will have to "cheat" by resorting to an open book for the answers. The book is the scriptures, which give insights into some of life's deepest secrets and mysteries.

God is Love. (1 Jn 4:16)

Love is God, without beginning and without end. God is all-good, forever pouring out goodness. God can't do anything else. It's impossible for God to run out of goodness and to stop giving. Conversely, it's impossible for God to do anything which is not good or which is bad. Love can do only what is good.

St. Paul is specific: "Love (or God) is always patient and kind, and never jealous. Love (or God) is never boastful or conceited; never rude or selfish. Love (or God) never takes offense and is not resentful. Love (or God) takes no pleasure in people's sins but delights in the truth (that everyone is precious). Love (or God) is always ready to excuse, to trust, to hope, and to endure whatever comes. Love (or God) never comes to an end." (1 Cor 13:4-8)

The amazing fact is that I am made in God's image. This means that I am created out of God's love in order to love and, of course, to be loved. The more I love, then, the closer I approach to being Godlike. The result is that I share more abundantly in the beatific joy that is God's nature.

Jesus is the beloved Son of God who describes his own loving mission as the Messiah:

"The blind see again, the lame walk, lepers are cleansed, the deaf hear and the dead are raised to life. The Good News (that God is Love) is proclaimed to the poor…" (Lk 7: 22) Jesus' whole life can be described simply, "He went about doing good." He said, "I have come so that they may have life and have it to the full." (Jn 10:10) "As the Father has loved me, so I have loved you… I have told you this so that my joy may be in you and your joy may be complete." (Jn 15:9-11)

For Love to be Love, it first of all must be freely done. It can't be forced or legislated. I have to want and choose to do the good for someone, starting with myself. That is the real power and beauty of Love. "God loved us with so much love that he was generous with his mercy: when we were dead through our sins, he brought us to life with Christ—it is through grace that you have been saved—and raised us up with him and given us a place with him in heaven…It is by grace that you have been saved, not by anything of your own, but by a gift from God; not by anything you have done, so that nobody can claim the credit. We are God's work of art, created in Christ Jesus to live the good life as from the beginning he has meant us to live it." (Eph 2:4-10)

In the story of the traveler and the old monk, I wonder what the old man would have done if the stranger had strong-armed him and stolen the jewel? What would happen to the spirit, then?

To illustrate the craziness of Love, Jesus says that the old monk should love and forgive the thug. For any harm done to me, I am to react with Love! Then I will be a child of the Most High God (Love), who is kind to the ungrateful and the wicked. (Lk 6:35) After all, Love can do only what is good.

This is exactly what Jesus did as he hung on the cross, wracked in pain and bleeding his last ounce of blood. "Father, forgive them. They do not know what they are doing. " (Lk 23:34).

But what is the sense of this extreme behavior? "I have told you this so that my own joy may be in you and your joy may be complete. This is my commandment: love one another, as I have loved you. One can have no greater love than to lay down his life for his friends." (Jn 15:11-13)

The commandment is not a new law Jesus is imposing on me and the world. He is simply enunciating the law of my nature and of everyone who exists, reminding me that I am made in the image of his Father. I am created to love. Marvelous!

People come in different delicious flavors: chocolate, vanilla, walnut, and lemon lime.

A Kingdom of Kids

"The Kingdom of God belongs to them..." (Lk 18:17)

Little Johnny came running into the house, back with his father from having checked out a new litter of kittens at a neighbor's house. Gasping with excitement he reported to his mother: "Mom, there were two boy kitties and two girl ones!"

"How do you know that?" his mom asked.

"Well, dad checked each one underneath," Johnny answered gravely. "I think it's printed on the bottom."

Kids say the most beguiling things, in all seriousness. Their little brains take giant, fanciful leaps as they try to unravel life's mysterious goings-on.

Here is a sampling of prayers by children. With such appeals as these ascending heavenward, how can God refuse?

"Dear God, if you really want to stop Cain from killing Abel and stuff like that, try giving them separate bedrooms. It worked with my brother and me."

"Thank you for my new baby brother, God. But, you know, I was really hoping for a puppy."

I imagine that these were the kinds of things the kids were doing and saying in an ancient town where the villagers brought their little ones to Jesus. When the apostles showed their annoyance and shooed them away, Jesus corrected–in fact, scolded them:

"Stop that! Leave the children alone. Don't chase them away, because the kingdom of heaven is made up of such as these." (Mk 10:13-16) Then Jesus began snuggling and caressing them, tossing them into the air, causing them to giggle with glee, teasing and playing the clown for them before kissing them and sending them off to play. Farfetched? I doubt it.

One day a kind, anonymous person left me the following copy of Danny Dutton's theology. It is such an enchanting statement that I can't resist sharing it with you. Danny must surely be a real person, because his statement rings with the authenticity of a little person, wafting pure simplicity and the sincerity of true wisdom. This was written to fulfill a third-grade homework assignment: "Explain God."

"One of God's main jobs is making people. He makes them to replace the ones that die so there will be enough people to take care of things here on earth. He doesn't make grown-ups, just babies. I think because they are smaller and easier to make. That way, he doesn't have to take up valuable time teaching them to talk and walk. He can just leave that to mothers and fathers.

God's second most important job is listening to prayers. An awful lot of this goes on, since some people, like preachers and things, pray at times besides bedtime. God doesn't have time to listen to the radio or TV on account of this.

Since God hears everything, not only prayers, there must be a terrible lot of noise in his ears, unless he has a way to turn it off.

God sees everything and hears everything, and is everywhere, which keeps him pretty busy. So you shouldn't go wasting his time by going over your parents' head, asking for something they said you couldn't have.

Atheists are people who don't believe in God. I don't think there are any in Chula Vista. At least there aren't any who come to our church. Jesus is God's Son. He used to do all the hard work like walking on water and performing miracles and trying to teach the people who didn't want to learn about God. They finally got tired of Him preaching to them and they crucified him. But he was good and kind like his Father, and he told his Father that they didn't know what they were doing and to forgive them, and God said OK. his Dad (God) appreciated everything that he had done and all his hard work on earth, so he told him he didn't have to go out on the road anymore. He could stay in Heaven. So he did.

And now he helps his Dad out by listening to prayers and seeing things which are important for God to take care of and which ones he can take care of himself without having to bother God. You can pray anytime you want, they are sure to hear you because they got it worked out so one of them is on duty a11 the time.

You should always go to church on Sunday because it makes God happy. And if there's anyone you want to make happy, it's God. Don't skip church to do something you think will be more fun like going to the beach. This is wrong! And besides, the sun doesn't come out at the beach on Sunday until noon, anyway.

If you don't believe in God, besides being an atheist, you will be very lonely, because your parents can't go everywhere with you, like to camp, but God can.

It's good to know he's around when you are scared in the dark or when you can't swim very good and you get thrown into real deep water by big kids. But you shouldn't always think of what God can do for you. I figure God put me here and he can take me back anytime he pleases. And that's why I believe in God."

–Danny Dutton, age 8, Chula Vista, CA.

For little ones, the hymn "Gladly the Cross I'd Bear" becomes "Gladly, the Cross-Eyed Bear" and Pontius Pilate becomes Pontius the Pilot. But who cares? I can picture the Father with tears in His eyes, howling a thunderous belly laugh with each childish malaprop.

Jesus took a little child, placed him in the center of his apostles and then wrapped his arms around the little one. He said, "Anyone who welcomes one of these little children in my name, welcomes me; and anyone who welcomes me welcomes the One who sent me." (Mk 9:37) "Unless you change–give up your silly fears and pompous self-importance–and become like little children you will never enter the kingdom of heaven," Jesus said. "Anyone who makes himself like this little child is the greatest in the kingdom of heaven. (Mt 18:3)

It was conceit and arrogance that brought Lucifer down, thinking that to be like God was to be bloated with pride and to wield vast power. But it turns out that our God is self-effacing and benevolent, our kind and loving Father who spoils and indulges us.

In fact, Jesus means to tell us that is the reason God created us. The Father is not a haughty potentate issuing orders from on high and lashing out angrily. Rather God is our Abba–that is, our Papa–and we are his children, his kids! So we can run to our Papa, wholly confident and unafraid, climb into his lap and play with him freely, just as the children did with Jesus. That, I'm sure, is the meaning of "enjoying the freedom and the glory of the children of God." (Rm 8:22) This is the heart and essence of the Good News.

Now one more story for good measure. Little Tommy was at the mall with his mother shopping endlessly. Suddenly in desperation, he cried out loud, "Mommy, I've got to pee!" Red-faced and embarrassed, his mother bent down and hissed, "Don't use that word when we are out in public like this. Say, "I have to whisper." Weeks later, Tommy was out with his grandpa when the urge struck again. "Grandpa, I have to whisper." Grandpa bent down and said, "All right, son. You can whisper in my ear."

What was that thunderous belly laugh up in the sky?

How blessed are the eyes that do not see – a difference.

The Gift of Blindness

What was Markie, my little nephew, doing here? As I was strolling with a friend in the Los Angeles arboretum, he came running toward me. When he drew up close I discovered that it wasn't Markie, after all. It was a boy who looked like him. He was afflicted with Down's syndrome, just like Markie, so there was a remarkable similarity between them.

In spite of never having met before, this little fellow, with arms flung wide, ran up to me, smiled and hugged me, a complete stranger. Why, that's exactly what Markie does with everyone he meets, too.

When Markie was born and diagnosed with the malady, a deep sense of sadness and tragedy came over the family. Such an irregularity was considered a curse in Chinese culture. Less fortunate babies were often abandoned and offerings were made to the gods to spare the family from future like misfortunes.

My new, little friend in the park made me think of the shortsightedness of most people who are put off by the presence and the guttural sounds coming from him and others like him. Yet there was no denying the warmth and love he lavished so openly on me. In that wonderful way, he was truly different from those who walk past others, as if they don't exist. Naturally, I hugged and loved him back, as his parents stood by approvingly.

I'm convinced that attitudes of fear and distrust of strangers, especially when it flows from reasons of skin color, race, customs or religion, are taught to us. Perhaps it all began when innocent persons were once victimized or rejected by strangers. After that, it was safer simply to avoid or to ignore all unknown persons. And yet, in all honesty, I think that the times I have experienced a snub are infinitesimal, compared to my many happy encounters. I have discovered that, if I am friendly or appear to be, I usually am repaid with similar smiles and acceptance.

Clyde was the foreman of a work crew refurbishing our school building where I was the high school principal many years ago. With his short-cropped hair and easy smile, friendly Clyde strode around the building in his soiled white coveralls, surveying the work in progress. The religious sisters and priests on staff told how he liked to corner them and ask very direct, searching questions like: "Do you really shave all your hair off, sister?" or "Don't you miss not being married and having a family?"

In my office he was at home chatting freely. He had never been so close to real nuns and priests before. He came originally from the deep South and had heard all kinds of wild and sordid things about the lifestyles of priests and nuns. Now he had the chance to find out for himself if the tall tales he had heard before were true. He was like a little boy in a classroom, curious and guileless.

He told me that it was only after he had come west that his eyes were fully opened as regards black folk. One day he was eating his bag lunch with a white buddy on one side of a mound of dirt, while black workers sat on the opposite side. "And you know what?" Clyde asked rhetorically, "They were talking about the same things we talk about: their love life, their homes, wives and kids, their plans and hopes! Why, they were just like us!"

He went on, getting wound up, as he recalled details of his background. "When we were growing up, we all thought that blacks were no better than dogs..." He went on with a litany of segregation laws and customs designed to keep blacks from contact with whites: separate restrooms, drinking fountains, riding in the back of buses and on and on.

Like Clyde, many have finally recognized the insidiousness of bigotry and the baseless stupidity of it all. Since the civil rights movement and desegregation, much healthier attitudes and practices have replaced the previous inhuman acts of prejudice.

And yet, many ugly forms of discrimination and prejudice continue to plague the human race. What the world needs is more Markies, blind to all the superficial differences that distinguish one person from another, having an abundance of love in search of persons on whom to lavish it.

Black is beautiful.

It's all right

Mary had a little lamb
Whose fleece was white as snow.
The prophet John proclaimed:
"This is the Lamb of God
Whose death will change
The crimson, scarlet sins of all
To wool's most dazzling white,
The shade of joy and mercy,
Love and peace."

About Birds and Bees and Humans

When I was about ten years old and the facts about the birds and the bees, as well as humans, were still a mystery to me, I encountered a type of woman I was yet to understand. One late afternoon, five of my siblings and cousins and I were headed to the Chinese school where we had classes beginning at five p.m. and lasting for three hours each evening. We had already finished our American school elementary classes at St. Mary's, as well as the bologna sandwiches mom always had prepared and which were awaiting us at our dad's grocery warehouse. The store and school were in the middle of a district that included the city's wholesale produce market, a Chinatown of sorts, some low-rent hotels and clapboard houses.

On this particular day, as we walked past one house, a middle-aged painted woman seated at a curtained window began tapping on the pane with her ring, while earnestly beckoning my brother Tom and cousin Frank to come in. Both were about sixteen years old. Instead of responding, they looked away and kept walking ahead. When I wondered aloud to them what she might have wanted, neither of them offered any explanation.

Only in my later years have I concluded that Phoenix in those days was still a wide-open frontier town in need of tighter laws and supervision.

Or perhaps, as in more progressive states like Nevada, the city could yield to "enlightened" attitudes to ease the restrictions that some believe reflect a puritanical attitude toward prostitution. It is, after all, a "victimless" crime, as proponents keep saying.

I am amazed at the efforts of so many otherwise intelligent people who seriously advocate legalizing, even promoting, what is inherently a degrading practice. After all, the argument goes, "the world's oldest profession" will never be eradicated. And yet, no matter how film and literature portray prostitutes as "Jezebels with golden hearts," "comfort women," or the glib and funny Mae West type, there is no denying the ultimate devastating effect on women who are slaves to prostitution.

How else can I explain the whispered suggestion of a cabby who was ferrying me to a hotel in Hong Kong, "You want pretty girl?" For the hotel, a neat profit; for the cabby, a slice of the pie. For the customer, selfish gratification; all at the expense of the girl, whose cash compensation can never buy back her dignity and self-esteem.

So, where's the crime? Anything that dehumanizes or debases a person, no matter how willing, is by that very fact evil. Every human being is a child of God and made in God's image to be free and happy. Prostitutes are usually the "property" of pimps or madams who control and subject them to every form of indignity and abuse for their self-aggrandizement. Servitude, whether under the dominance of others or to one's own weaknesses, destroys peace and happiness.

So many chance encounters in life are branded in my memory. Once when I was en route to a parish engagement in Reno, our entire flight was fully booked, except for the aisle seat next to mine—an unusual stroke of good luck. The cabin had already been secured as we readied for takeoff. Suddenly, the door opened, admitting a final passenger who came vociferously down the aisle.

He was so raucous that everyone was forced to listen to his prattling. He crashed into the empty seat next to me and slapped me on the thigh. He held out his hand in a friendly gesture as his voice boomed, "Hi, I'm Joe. What's your name?"

It was an effort to speak softly, so as not to burden fellow passengers with our small talk. Still in his loud voice, he insisted on asking, "You on business or pleasure?" When I quietly said it was a business trip, he said, "Too bad. I'm out here for fun, man, fun."

He lapsed into a monologue revealing that he was a building contractor on a break from South Carolina, vacationing separately from his wife by mutual agreement, blah, blah. Then in a quiet moment he pulled out a notebook to check on a list of planned activities while visiting his fantasyland. From the corner of my eye—shame on me—I could make out the scribbled names of several well-known hotels, casinos and shows. At the bottom of the list the name "Mustang Ranch" jumped out clearly. It is arguably the most notorious brothel in a state where prostitution is legalized.

Leaning toward me and digging his elbow into my side, he whispered, "Say, what do you know about Mustang Ranch?" What could I do but shrug and say, "Not much"?

We landed, mercifully, and walked together to the baggage claim. There several greeters from the parish ran up to meet me. "Welcome, father!" they exclaimed, and threw their arms around me. I looked up as Joe stood there, a stunned look on his face.

Believe it or not, he sheepishly sidled up to me and asked, "What do you think of me?" I merely shrugged my shoulder.

"It doesn't matter what I think, Joe. Have a good time."

I often wonder if he finally got to the Ranch and, if he did, was it really the fun he had expected?

Whether my friend Joe eventually made it to the brothel or not, I would be willing to bet that, if it had been Jesus on board the plane, he would have been heading there without any embarrassment at all. In fact, Christ was constantly criticized for "hanging out" with and befriending social outcasts like prostitutes, criminals and unclean defectives. That's because his life's passion and purpose was to search for such kind. He had a message for them that would give them back their self-worth and a noble sense of direction.

"If you had a flock of a hundred sheep," he asked a crowd of people, including his critics, "and one of them is lost, wouldn't you leave the rest to fend for themselves and go search for the missing stray?" To which all appeared simply to shake their heads. What's one sheep, more or less? It makes no sense to jeopardize the rest of the flock by leaving them unguarded. All were contemptuous skeptics, except for an attractive woman standing on the fringe of the crowd, unrecognized behind her veiled face. She was the town prostitute, reviled and despised. This man named Jesus who radiated such authority and charm mesmerized her. (Lk 15:1-10)

"When a shepherd finally locates the missing lamb," Jesus went on, "he jubilantly calls all his friends over to celebrate his good fortune with him. Well, it's the same in heaven. There is more rejoicing there over the recovery of one single, wayward person than over ninety-nine who have never wandered or failed." The woman's heart beat hard with hope, as she pondered this news.

The point of Jesus is unavoidable: every person is like pure gold, precious, and bad behavior never diminishes one's intrinsic worth.

It's no wonder then that, when Jesus was invited later to dine with a prominent Pharisee, the pretty woman of ill repute learned of it and came in uninvited and unwelcome by the host. The stunned guests watched in amazement as this scarlet woman knelt at the feet of Jesus. Her body shook with sobbing and her river of tears bathed his dusty feet. Letting her long hair fall loose she wiped his feet dry. She kissed them again and again and then poured a precious nard ointment over them, and its fragrance filled the room.

Jesus made it clear, "She has made many mistakes, but her many sins must have been forgiven or she would not be showing such great love and gratitude."

"Your sins are all forgiven," he said to her. "Be at peace. It's your deepest conviction that reminds you of how precious you are and saves you from guilt and the fear of unworthiness."

In all the gospels one certain woman stands out prominently besides Mary, the mother of Jesus—each of them at opposite ends of the virtue spectrum. It is another Mary, the notorious prostitute from Magdala, who is one of Jesus' closest friends. She stands as a shining symbol of salvation history. It was from her that Jesus had cast out seven demons. And it was her tenacious, grateful love that brought her to his tomb with fragrances on Easter morning. Her reward was to be the first person to see him alive again—and fittingly, as she herself had been brought back to life, too!

Love is the only gift everyone needs & can afford.

*First, a taut, bleached canvas...
  Then an unseen artist paints a masterpiece - each spring.*

Recycling Paper, Bottles & Souls

"Who of you, if you had a hundred sheep and one strayed, would not leave the ninety-nine in the wilds and search until he found the lost one?"

(Lk 15:4)

A newly-arrived friend from South America—this is a true story except for the appropriate name change—enrolled in a local university to earn her teaching degree. Needing funds, Inocencia responded to an ad for a sales person in a bookstore. Calling ahead, she spoke to a representative and asked that he hold the position open for her.

At the proper address she found the place eerily strange. Even the clerk who met her seemed shifty-eyed and peculiar. He left the room to summon the manager. By now, Inocencia's eyes had adjusted to the low-lighted room, in harsh contrast to the brilliant sunlight outside. To her dismay, her wide eyes took in display racks and whole walls lined with garish magazines flaunting nude male and female bodies in obscene poses. In the display counter on which she was leaning was an array of artificial genitalia and assorted erotic paraphernalia.

She gasped in panic and ran for the exit. Flushed with shame, she shuddered and glanced up and down the street to see if anyone had seen her entering. She fought the urge to throw up.

Inocencia had of course stepped into an adult bookstore. Ugh! Her skin crawled. She felt so dirty. Contaminated. Guilty.

Ironically, were Jesus physically present today, I would probably find him in that sleazy bookstore, or a topless bar and even worse places. He wouldn't be there by accident but actually by choice, not to buy salacious trash but to befriend the misguided sellers and "entertainers."

"He fraternized with sinners…" (Mk 2:16) Jesus was constantly criticized and condemned for hanging out with the human litter of society. The company he kept did not seem appropriate for someone who was reputedly the Messiah.

So it was to the consternation of all his critics that he purposefully sought out society's lowlifes. He knew the great possibilities in each and every person, no matter how creepy they might appear. He would find a way to inspire them to rise from the mire of wasted lives and reach for loftier goals.

It is not by chance that Mary Magdalen, the reputed harlot, plays such a prominent role in the gospel story. Hers is the case of someone who was lifted from the dregs by Jesus' friendship to become a paragon of goodness and hope to anyone weighed down and trapped by vice and addictions. In fact, she was the first person privileged to meet the Risen Christ on that brilliant Easter Sunday morning and to tell the world that Jesus had overpowered death itself.

"I have not come to condemn the world, but to save the world." (Jn 12:47): "I came that they might have life and have it abundantly." (Jn 10:10) If only I shared with Jesus that same zeal and open-hearted love for others.

I was once invited to conduct a prayer service with the staff of Goodwill Industries in Los Angeles. When I arrived and went upstairs to the fifth floor of their multi-storied building in the industrial district, I looked down on the street below. People were streaming into the building from every direction, after being disgorged from public buses. But it was not your ordinary crush of commuters. These people were arriving in wheelchairs or limping on crutches or canes, some of them blind or armless, each one in some way handicapped. It was a scene right out of a Charles Dickens novel. I was fascinated.

I thought of them as I prayed. Each disabled person in the group had been in some way discarded from the ordinary work force as non-productive or at least an economic liability not worth hiring. Today, however, they had arrived like anyone else reporting for work. In a moment they would all disperse to different parts of the building to start their duties.

A supervisor escorted me on a tour of the facility. Starting at the dock we watched large trucks arriving from their pickups around the city. Piles were unloaded of what most people would consider worthless junk: broken lamps, stoves, chairs, divans, mattresses, curtains, blankets, shoes, toasters, clothes hangers by the thousands and loose articles of clothing of every size, shape and color. As this chaotic mess rolled by, sorters stationed along the conveyer belt separated the items into proper heaps by categories. Obviously donors had not been particularly careful about depositing things that were clean and neat.

Depending on the nature of the articles, transporters delivered the collections to various floors for repair and reconditioning by specialists. There were carpenters and plumbers, laundresses and seamstresses, tinkerers and general fixit workers, all busy at work. The most quaint and charming scene I remember was a corner occupied by a round little man, pipe in mouth, surrounded by hundreds of clocks of every size and shape ticking and tocking. This was his little world where his skill made him king.

The entire operation left an unforgettable impression on me. Here I was witnessing a deeply moving, living panorama of reclaimed human beings who were industriously reclaiming and renewing discarded things to be made useful once again.

"Bless each of these workers, dear God," I prayed, "with good health and the deep satisfaction that comes from doing what will benefit so many others who are less fortunate…"

"Those who do not forgive destroy the bridge over which they might one day need to pass."

Forgiveness: The Highest Love

In his book "Without Feathers," Woody Allen the humorist isn't sure there is a God. "If there is a God," he asks, "how do you account for famine and daytime television?" He can be hilariously profound as he blends the serious with the absurd. So messed up is our world that, to make his point, Allen skirts blasphemy while blaming God for the world's chaos and suggesting he must be an "underachiever."

How can life's wretchedness be explained in the light of God's omnipotence? In the process of creation, why didn't the all-powerful God arrange for peace and harmony on earth? That having failed, why doesn't God straighten everything out now and prove his existence beyond all doubt? Woody Allen speaks for all the skeptics: "If only God would give me some clear sign (of his existence), like making a large deposit in my name at a Swiss bank."

A glance at the news confirms Woody Allen's gloomy evaluation. For somewhere at this moment bloody wars are raging in place of rational settling of differences. There are fierce struggles for liberation by the oppressed or heartrending cries of unfortunate millions dying from disease and starvation. Meantime, in the halls of power, fraud and corruption have become "fine arts."

And yet, if all these sores on humanity's body were healed by tonight, there would not necessarily be peace in our lives. Other large problems lie closer to home. Desertions and divorce, along with their implied hatred and violence, make a mockery of the ideal and sanctity of marriage. Scandalous accounts of child abuse among clergy crowd the news.

These are but a few of the frightful symptoms of a prevailing domestic sickness.

More and more the evidence points to the ugliness in ordinary people like ourselves which turns communities into hell. We're all acquainted with the contorted caricatures of human relationships: the curled-lip snarl; the you-stupid-idiot sneer; the I'll get-even glower; the go-to-hell sulk.

Clearly all these ugly faces were not made by God. They are all made by out-of-joint humans who can't even say honestly, "The devil made me do it." And the only way the ugly faces will disappear is when the wearers decide to get rid of them.

Why are so many people filled with hatred and revenge? To begin with, vindictive people possibly expect too much of others. Humans are, after all, human- which implies that they are capable of and, as experience shows, inclined to do wrong. Once admitted, this realization ought to temper our expectations. We should not become unglued over someone's mistakes, including our own. Above all, we will not be so reluctant to forgive.

Closer to home, each of us without exception has an assortment of personal wrongs, both secret and known. This is as sure as there is a God. How then can anyone have the consummate gall to hold another person to a flawless life? Why not, rather, expect to be disappointed by others since, sooner or later, we are quite certain to be?

This attitude is not to be negativistic; it is to be realistic. To admit our human tendency toward wrongdoing is not a put-down of human beings; it is to accept ourselves as we truly are. And paradoxically, this very tendency to do wrong underscores our need for one another. Because nowhere else is it so obvious that humans depend on each other than in their mutual need for forgiveness.

Out of human failure spring instances of the most marvelous human qualities: mercy and understanding, patience and pardon, compassion and reconciliation. The essence of being a unique individual consists in this: that each person possesses powers entirely his/her own. One God-like power each one possesses is the ability to forgive without conditions and freely to love another person, no matter how undeserving. To do this makes a person truly human and truly divine.

Forgiveness yields sweet rewards of peace and fresh beginnings. The kiss of lovers making up is far more soothing and downright fun than if they had never had a tiff or falling out.

Those who refuse to forgive trump up endless alibis, usually reducible to a false sense of righteousness and superiority over the wrongdoers. Absolute judgments flow like water: "They're scum. You can't trust them," "She'll never change,' "He's a rotten rat,' "He hurt me once too often and he can't be believed," "It's in their blood." Unforgiving people pass sentence on their enemies and label them irreversibly. They strip offenders of even the possibility of remorse, literally kicking them while they're down and, for good measure, burying their heels in their backs.

Every Christmas two sisters of Polish extraction send me greetings, along with a thin sheet of ornamented unleavened bread. It is the old custom of Upwatek or *Vigilia*, when families gather on Christmas Eve. In a touching ceremony, each one, from father and mother to the youngest child, admits his or her injuries to the others during the past year and then asks for forgiveness of them. The climax arrives when all consume a piece of the bread, symbolizing their grievances and hurts, embrace each other and then pledge to start the new year together in mutual love and respect.

If only every family would schedule something similar into their traditions…

This then is the process. To acknowledge that everyone has done and will continue to make mistakes. And yet no person is so bad that he or she cannot be forgiven. Each of us has the power to decide: do I forgive or don't I? This is ever the question and the challenge. For the whole world will be blown to cinders and people will finally wipe themselves out, if their only recourse is to retaliate.

To think of a wrongdoer as one who has fallen, and that the helping hand held out to him enables him to rise and to grow to full potential, is to love him. Our God-given instructions are precisely to love another, especially an "enemy"- that is, one who has abused you. To love an enemy is the ultimate act of human dignity. For by doing so, one transforms the enemy into a friend.

Woody Allen and other buck-passers try to make God the goat for the world's problems. But peace on earth, the harmony between peoples, will come only when each of us chooses to make it come.

Those who do not forgive destroy the bridge over which they may one day need to pass.

This was the sixth of a seven-part Lenten series that first appeared in the National Catholic Reporter, 1977. Reprinted by permission.

Your greatest strentgh is your gentleness.

When Weak is Strong

When liturgists concocted the "anamnesis" following the words of consecration, one was sure it was a stolen medical term for the Asian flu. Ecclesiology is church talk, seldom heard anywhere other than sacred surroundings and just as irrelevant to simple folk. So religious malaprops with mangled meanings abound, as for instance: homily—a southern food; humility—a low opinion of yourself; Lent-the fuzzy stuff under your bed.

Even Jesus himself suffers in "translation." For example, a bumper sticker, obviously copying from Coke, says to "Enjoy Jesus, the Real Thing." And that's exactly what he means to many: sticky sweet, goody-good, somewhat effeminate and, oh yes, don't forget to "Honk, if you love Jesus."

In his day, people imposed their own meanings on Jesus, too. On Palm Sunday, he thrilled to their cheers of "Hosanna! Blessings on the King of Israel who comes in the name of the Lord!" But for the crowd, this miracle-worker who effortlessly multiplied loaves, changed water into wine, cured diseases and raised the dead was a "natural" to be the messiah and champion who would free them from hated Roman tyrants. Then the liberated Jews could strut around as arrogantly and contemptuously as the Egyptians, Babylonians and Romans who had ground them into the dirt for centuries.

Knowing this, Jesus dodged the glory-seekers, for his kingdom was "not from here," - not one of pomp and power, pride and prestige. At Jesus' mock trial, the jealous Pharisees turned their own frustrated ambitions against their unwilling hero who, they lied, was attempting to subvert the Romans. "Are you a king?" Pilate asked, not a little worried.

"You're right," Jesus said, "I am a king. I was born for this. I came into the world for this: to bear witness to the truth. All who are on the side of truth listen to my voice." (Jn 18:37)

"Truth?" Pilate sniffed. "What is that?" After all, how could so self-serving a worldling be expected to know the answer?

For glory-hounds, "king" meant only power and dominance over others. For Christ, it meant rather to be the paragon of one who testified to the truth. And that is "true" which is in conformity with the heavenly Father's will. To be king did not mean wearing a crown but fulfilling his Father's plan faithfully and totally.

The Father asks our willing conversion and loving surrender. We are invited to work with him. With Christ, we are commissioned to help build the kingdom of God on earth. The kingdom is composed of those who live and act by Christ's pattern of obedience to the Father's will. Only thus can there be peace, harmony, mercy and compassion, justice and friendship, forgiveness and love.

The universe is God's, created to function in harmony and coordination. Until every person is contributing and receiving love and service, mercy and forgiveness, healing and compassion, the kingdom of God has not come.

At first sight, this King Jesus is an embarrassing letdown and flop. Instead of galloping into the city, astride a magnificent charger, helmeted, with cape flowing in the wind, he comes on a flop eared, trudging jackass! No soldiers marching in phalanx, no trumpets blaring. Only peasants and beggars in his entourage.

And when they capture him later, he seems gutless and without honor, not putting up a fight and smashing his captors in self-defense. He's a sissy. He stands there while they mock him, cough their spit into his face, slap and whip him mercilessly.

And now here's the so-called son of God writhing like a worm, spiked through his hands and feet to two crossed poles, naked and exposed to the world, abandoned by all but a loyal couple. What a comedown. He's a pitiful fool, after all.

But wait a minute! What is the clown on the cross saying? Listen. "Father, forgive them. They don't know what they are doing."

"Forgive them?" This loser Jesus must be crazy from the heat and pain. Now is when he ought to open the earth and swallow up the goons who are tormenting him.

That's undoubtedly what we would say and do. We always have to come out on top. We can't have egg on our face. It's un-American.

But that's the difference between Jesus King and us. To that extent, we haven't listened to him and accepted what he has said over and over again. He is now practicing what he has been preaching all his life.

"I say this to you who are listening: love your enemies. Do good to those who treat you badly. If someone slaps you on one cheek, offer the other cheek too. Give to everyone who asks you, and do not ask for your property back from one who robs you." (Lk 6:27)

This is not empty theologizing. This is the heart of the gospel. No one can escape its inexorable application. Therefore: those who see no alternative to execution of criminals ought to reconsider. Spouses devastated by their partners' indiscretions ought to reconsider. Parents gravely grieved by son or daughter ought to reconsider. Those who have been robbed ought to reconsider. Church authorities who hold the fate and consciences of so many in their official hands ought to reconsider. Any person, in whatever way offended, mistreated, insulted, injured or crushed by others ought to reconsider.

To see in every predicament of life a plan and purpose; to search for meaning and value in the bitter, inescapable traps of life; to be willing to cope with sickness, disability and setbacks—not fatalistically and without hope, but trusting unswervingly in our loving Father who will not allow us to be destroyed—this is to be converted and to surrender to His will.

This is what that sissy Jesus did. "He emptied himself and took the form of a slave." (Phil 2:6) Ours would be a totally different world of compassion and understanding, if all people were such sissies who refused to trade evil for evil. This kind of weakness is stronger than steel. Jesus, it turns out, is tough. He has the stuff of a real king. He loved us. So he freely and willingly died for us on a cross.

> *But God raised him high and gave him the name*
> *Which is above all other names;*
> *So that all beings in the heavens, on earth and the underworld,*
> *Should bend their knee at the name of Jesus*
> *And every tongue should acclaim Jesus Christ as Lord-and King-*
> *To the glory of God the Father. (Phil 12:9-11)*

Long live Jesus Christ - KING!

This was the seventh of a seven-part Lenten series that first appeared in the National Catholic Reporter, 1977.
Reprinted by permission.

Thorns have roses.

Must Joy always bring Twin Sister, Pain, Along?

MaryPat's letter brought a lump of sadness to my throat. "This morning my 59-year old father prepares for a bone scan. His PSA count has accelerated, and the doctors suspect his cancer has returned. What do I pray for? I am the oldest of six children, ages 36 to 25. We're what you would call a young lot. Is 59 years as full a life as 99? His mother, you see, just celebrated her 97th birthday. Her husband, daughter, even a great-grandchild have died before her. She wonders why God has let her "hang on." And what about my mother? She's angry with my father for putting off the cancer test, being afraid of the future. They are both alive with God's love, but I know they are trying to understand the meaning of this suffering in their lives. Can you help me understand and deal with this awful pain and anxiety?"

I'm stumped. I can't be glib. Of all the problems of life, the evils of pain and suffering are the hardest for me to comprehend. Unpredictable but certain, they come unannounced, like vicious intruders who break in, turn a house upside down and leave chaos in their wake. Pain and suffering are as sure as the sunrise, sparing no one. Depending on the hurt, the question "Why?" is asked in agonizing screams or soft whimpering. Or "Why me?", as if implying the pain were better if visited on someone else.

When a catastrophic illness strikes, it's often traceable to an errant virus or bacterium, a carcinogen or other detectable cause. Horrendous traffic accidents, however, may have resulted from human error, drugs or drink. Even unspeakable crimes of torture and rape, assault and murder are acts of humans, which can and should be controlled. To a certain extent, this brand of evil can at least be mitigated, if not totally eliminated.

But sometimes it is the broken spirits and bodies of innocent children, a dear relative or even the anguished face of an anonymous, maimed victim on a magazine cover—or I myself—who must bear the perpetual scars of misfortune. Why did it happen?

When cataclysmic evil strikes in a litany of horrific hurricanes, tornadoes and earthquakes, fires and floods, famines and plagues, they are dubbed "acts of God." After all, no mere human power can cause such fury and devastation. Once more I must ask, why?

Is God angry and vindictive? Is this due to some almighty pout? Is God punishing his wayward creatures or, at the very least, just testing their endurance and faith on a rack of pain? As an impressionable youngster I was fed such facile explanations and swallowed them whole without question. Righteous fingers were wagged at me, warning that God will not be mocked and will punish with justice every iota of unruly behavior by disobedient creatures. It kept me in line—somewhat. But it's no wonder I so often hear the cry of anguish following some terrible twist of fate, "What have I done to deserve this?"

I am increasingly annoyed when I hear frightened people express in absolute terms how God is angered by the misconduct of humans and wreaks havoc on them in retaliation. What childish nonsense. I can understand how ignorant cave dwellers fabricated mythological gods and demons that had to be humored to guarantee good fortune or else face catastrophe. Aztec priests offered up still-beating, bloody hearts of unlucky captives or drowned innocent maidens to placate hideous, grinning stone gods. Ghastly.

I can forgive them their ignorance; how could they know any better? Today mere school kids can explain the nature and origin of hurricanes and track their course. They will tell you that earthquakes are the movements of the earth's tectonic plates. Science has unraveled many mysteries of natural phenomena.

My impatience is directed against many so-called christians who should know better than to prate about God's vengeance displayed in natural phenomena. After all, we are two thousand years beyond the fulfillment of history's pivotal event, when all the prophecies given to the human race were fulfilled and God sent his Son into the world.

To terrorize? To punish? To exterminate? To avenge and pay God back for all the honor and glory stolen from him by pretentious, disobedient humans?

Listen to Jesus saying, "I have not come to condemn or to destroy. I have come to save what was lost. (Jn 12:47) I have come to feed my hungry sheep. I have come to tell you the truth about God, who is in fact your Abba (papa), and you are his children."

"When you make my word your home, (when you grasp the real meaning of the gospel Good News), you will know the truth, (and if you truly believe, you will discover the real God), and the truth will set you free—*free!*—from fear, guilt, anxiety. (Jn 8:31) Then, at last, little flock, you will discover and savor the peace that I have promised you from the beginning."

From such clear assurances, how can anyone persist in believing the opposite—namely, that ours is a vindictive, spiteful, petulant God, given to outbursts and fits of temper and violence?

Yet, how do I know for sure? With God and the unknowns of the future, I am challenged to accept certain convictions based on what has been revealed in scripture. The unseen God has been described to me in clear images as a loving Father, and I am his beloved child. He not only feeds the birds and dresses the flowers but has even counted the hairs on my head—a fairly easy task for him, in my case. I cling to this perception and play it over and over in my mind's eye. It comforts and strengthens me in my waking hours. It is my faith.

When I am steeped in this knowledge and relationship with God I have no problems in placing all my trust in God. Unlike humans, God is constant. Once God's word is given, it is set in stone and will never change.

Like others, I have tasted the bitterness of lies and human betrayal, making me cynical and wary of deceit and dishonesty. But with God's word, Jesus challenges me in the form of a declaration, "How happy and blessed are those who have not seen and yet believe!" (Jn 20:29)

Dear Jesus, Master, I do believe. But I admit that sometimes, when terrible things happen, I become anxious and afraid, even doubtful. Help my unbelief. Give me courage to believe all you have revealed and taught. Let me accept your challenge and never stop trusting you. Amen.

How blessed are the rich! They have so much to share..

In Deepest Gratitude

"We give you thanks, Almighty God, for these and all your gifts..."

In was a bright, sunny day. And we clergy looked festive in our embroidered vestments as we paraded down the aisle for the Thanksgiving Day liturgy. I looked out over the crowd that filled the church. Young and old, Caucasian, dark-skinned, Asian-a large mixed throng had come around the liturgical family table to express their gratitude this day. Many had brought bulging bags of food they piled at the base of the altar table, later to be passed out to needy families.

Today I was elected to be the homilist. But first the deacon proclaimed from St. Luke's gospel the story of the ten lepers who called out desperately to Jesus, pleading with him to heal them. He responded by sending them off to the temple priest, who had authority to determine whether they were ritually "unclean" or pure. While on their way, voila! each found himself completely healed and cleansed of his hideous malignancy!

But just one of them hurried back to Jesus to pour out his feelings of immense gratitude. (Lk 17.11-19)

I began my reflection focusing on the simple, humbling fact that, a hundred years ago, not one of us in this large gathering even existed. And that, a hundred years from this day, almost certainly, not a single one present–not even newborn babies, would still be living. What a sobering and scary thought!

Life is an amazing mystery. Like everyone else I awoke this morning, not because

I decided to; I just did. And each one hopes or even expects that the same awakening will happen tomorrow and tomorrow and tomorrow. And it will, unless something tragic happens to us or our allotted time has expired.

And then, what? Good question. After all, just as no one has decided to be born or to awaken each morning, what is going to happen when life ends?

Having no clue, some people are convinced that this mysterious, conscious existence called life simply ends, like a candlewick burned out. That is death. The End. Wipeout. Oblivion.

We believe differently. We're gathered today because of our shared conviction: we are what we are because of an unseen God who, for some mystical, marvelous reason, "chose us before the world began, to be holy and spotless, and to live in his presence through love." (Eph 1)

The scriptures are God's revelation, a peek behind the curtain of some of life's mysteries which, far from terrifying us, are filled with consolation and reassurance. "Don't let your hearts be troubled... I am the truth... I have come to give you peace," Jesus says comfortingly. (Jn 14 passim)

The thanks we voice in word and song today are a grand act of humility. We are expressing how limited and absolutely dependent we are. For without God's creative, loving and sustaining hand, we are nothing. And it all comes free.

St. Luke's story about the ten lepers, rotting and eaten away by their hideous disease, called out to Jesus to be healed. And he obliged all ten. But just one of them—an otherwise undeserving alien—came back to give thanks and to offer praise.

"Where are the other nine?" Jesus asked. "Weren't they healed, too?"

Was his question a pout of disappointment at not being thanked? Foolish question. Jesus isn't so small. After all, wasn't his healing a magnificent gesture of love, freely given?

Nor do I think the other nine were ingrates. I imagine they were just so giddy and excited to be healthy again that they simply ran home to celebrate their good fortune with family and friends. And no wonder. The cold, insensitive law had prohibited any contact with others while they were unclean. Then when their initial excitement wore off, they gradually resumed their normal life rhythm and routine like everyone else.

I imagine they were like most people who take life and all its gifts for granted. It's easy to do. People who are born beautiful or brainy, agile and athletic, or raised in comfort and plenty, tend to think they are self-made. Preening egotism is moral leprosy.

Thanksgiving Day should be a wakeup call. It's a reminder to everyone that "It is God who gives everything—including life and breath—to everyone." (Acts 17:27)

Why does God give so much? In a way, it's because God can't help it. Being Love itself, God literally has to give, lavishly. To everyone. No exceptions. And only what is good, wonderful, and beautiful. "The Father causes the rain to fall and the sun to shine on good and bad people alike." (Mt 5: 45)

One of the greatest revelations is the astounding fact that we are children of God, made in the image of God. I doubt that I look like God. But I am convinced that I can, in some small degree, emulate God's love by giving and sharing generously. "You received without charge, so give without charge." (Mt 10:8)

In that spirit, then, let me share with you a selection from a priest friend:

If you love something, set it free.

If it comes back, it will always be yours.

If it doesn't come back, it was never yours, to begin with.

But if it just sits in your living room,

Messes up your stuff,

Eats your food; uses your telephone, takes your money

And doesn't appear to realize that you have set it free.

You either married it or gave birth to it.

So what's wrong with that picture? Clearly, someone is behaving like a giant vacuum sweeper, selfishly sucking everything in and giving nothing but trouble.

Like the grateful leper we have all gathered together: whole families and individuals, to express thanks for having our needs met. Besides thanking God, the Ultimate Source of all Good, you children, be sure to thank your parents for all their sacrifices and loving care. And parents, remember to thank your children for the pride and joy they bring you.

Outside the family circle, don't forget the many people who do not have this day off: our overseas peacekeepers, our police and firefighters, our vigilant power and road maintenance crews—and so many countless other service persons who cater to our every need.

We can even thank the poor, the homeless and the helpless who, by their very needy condition, give us the opportunity to love and to share our bounty—like God. Say thanks and hand out sincere compliments for service and favors received. Simple praise or a pat on the back can brighten someone's day.

At table one day, a waitress handed me a compliment in a shy, breathless way. "Forgive me, sir, but I've been noticing how smooth and soft your skin looks! May I touch it?" Pleased and flattered, I replied with gusto, "Touch away, baby!"

Arms outstretched, the Church beckons, "Come to me, all you who are over-burdened and weary, and I will refresh you."

My Church

One day Jesus asked his disciples, "Who do people say I am?" (Mt 16:13-23) The question might have caught them off guard, but they managed to blurt out some weak guesses like: John the Baptizer, Elijah, Jeremiah or some other prophet. I can see Jesus shaking his head somewhat sadly. His followers still hadn't put two and two together, even after all the wonders he had been performing for their benefit.

"Well, how about you? Who do you think I am?" Jesus asked, while looking directly at his disciples. They probably fidgeted around and looked away, not too sure themselves.

"You are the messiah, Son of the living God!" Peter declared emphatically. Or did he declare it with the hint of doubt in his voice, adding, ""Aren't you?" I suggest this because of the sequence of events.

Jesus turned to Peter, nodding his approval, "You are blessed, Simon. You've got what no one else has been able to comprehend. My heavenly Father has conferred this wisdom on you directly. And now I am going to name you 'Petros'—the Rock. It is on this rock that I will build my church. The jaws of death—the gates of hell—shall never prevail over it. I will entrust to you the keys of the kingdom of heaven. And whatever you declare bound on earth will be bound in heaven; whatever you loose on earth will be loosed in heaven." (Mt 16:16-20)

What on earth was going through Peter's head as he heard those words addressed to him? After all, he and the others had been jockeying for the privileged positions around their Master, just as the mother of James and John had tried when she asked that her sons be seated at the left and right of Jesus "when he established his kingdom." (Mt 20:21) At this point the rest became incensed and elbowed them back, as if saying, "Get back there where you belong."

I think Peter moved to the front with a bit of a swagger, he who was chosen and appointed to be the head and leader of the kingdom by the Master himself. But what did he make of the "church" that Jesus referred to? After all, they had been dreaming of that mighty political state that their people had prayed for over the centuries, led by the Messiah. Jesus did not mention a temple or a synagogue; he spoke of a church, an assembly or community—a novel concept and certainly unclear.

· · · · · · · · ·

In the Book of Numbers Moses and Aaron, divinely appointed leaders of the Israelites in their torturous exodus, meet severe criticism from the community, which was unhappy with the shortages of food and water. "Why have you led us out of Egyptian captivity into this desert where we and our livestock are dying?" (Nm 20: 1-13) Moses and Aaron, fearful of an insurrection, pleaded with the Lord for a solution to their plight. Instructed to strike a designated rock that would yield life-saving waters, Moses, in a weak moment of doubt, struck it twice with his staff. Instantly, torrents of cool, clear waters gushed out to slake the thirst of the community and their flocks.

· · · · · · · · ·

This is the paradigm of my church, the rock from which stream the torrents of cool, refreshing life-giving waters. Waters that bathe tired, burning soiled feet and bodies and relieve aching, thirsty spirits. This is the image I associate with the gentle Shepherd who will leave a flock of ninety-nine to go in search of a single stray until he finds it. He is happier with finding the one lost sheep than over the ninety-nine obedient ones who remain together. It is God's plan that not a single one of the little ones should ever come to grief. (Mt 10:12-14)

The rock, then, is not a simile of the church in the sense of triumphalistic invulnerability, infallibility or eternity. Rather, my church is composed of weak, even sinful, people, ministering soothing relief and security with unlimited compassion and caring. When Peter is given the keys of the kingdom of love and peace, he is assured that whatever is loosed here on earth is loosed in heaven.

My dream is that the Church will always lovingly loosen all that holds God's people in bondage, in response to God's own plea as expressed in the gospel spiritual: "Let my people go."

When the disciples asked Jesus to teach them how to pray, he responded by expressing his dream of the goals of his kingdom:

The Jesus Dream

Our Father, unseen God in the heavens,
You are holy, kind and wonderful!
How we wish for your loving plan to become
as real on our earth as it is in heaven.
For then all will be healthy and fed
in body and in spirit;
All will be happy and satisfied.
For everyone is your child,
a daughter or a son,
precious and loved.
Help us to live together in peace,
forgiving each other's mistakes,
just as you hold nothing against us, ever .
And then we will have heaven on our earth. Amen.

Enough dreaming. Let's make it happen!

"Goodbye Grandma. Thank you for teaching us how to be thoughtful and loving of others..."

Keeping the Appointment

"You do not know the day nor the hour…" (Mt 25:13)

Some fellows were mulling over what had happened at a funeral they had just attended.

Joe: "What would you guys like to hear them saying about you, when you're lying in the coffin?"

Jim: "I'd sure like to hear them saying what a nice guy I'd been and that they were going to miss me a lot."

Fred: "Well, I'd like them to be recalling some of my accomplishments and successes."

Ernie: "What I'd like to hear them saying is, 'Hey! He's still moving!'"

· · · · · · · · ·

As a young seminarian I was spellbound by a preacher at our annual post-Christmas retreat. My jaw was agape as I hung on every word of a disturbing legend:

"A courtier was happily sauntering along a corridor in the palace when he pulled up short. There in front of him stood the shrouded figure of Death itself! The courtier froze in his tracks, rubbed his eyes and blinked incredulously. He gulped hard, spun around and dashed at breakneck speed down the long corridor, right into the royal chamber.

"Milord, milord," he gasped. Stuttering uncontrollably, he managed to sputter out a request. "H-h-have I b-b-been a faithful servant?"

"Yes, I suppose so," the king drew out his reply, wondering what could be causing the courtier such agitation.

"M-m-may I ask a favor of you, sire?"

"Of course, what is it?" was the king's instant response.

"M-m-may I borrow the fastest horse in the royal stables?"

"Yes, you have my permission. Go and take it. Return as soon as you can."

Leaping on the horse the courtier rode madly the whole day through the hot desert, beating furiously on the poor horse. Finally, as the sun was setting, he reached a distant walled city and dashed across the drawbridge, just as it was being raised. Breathless, he mopped his brow and headed toward a drinking fountain. Suddenly he froze in his tracks. There in front of him stood the same sinister black shrouded figure of Death!

The courtier's head slumped to his heaving chest. At last he looked up. "Didn't I see you at my master's palace this morning?"

"That is correct,' nodded Death ominously, "and, to tell you the truth, I was quite puzzled. I knew my assignment was to meet you here this night. But when I met you back there so far away I wondered how you could possibly be here where I was told to meet you. Thank you for your efforts. Come, let us go."

That was only a legend, fiction at its best. What follows, however, is true and, in a sense, even stranger and more chilling than fiction.

I was scheduled to direct a day of recollection at Serra Retreat in Malibu with a group of ladies recruited by Mary, a very active retreatant. The seasonal rains that year had drenched the hills, and mudslides made the highway nearly impassable. So I kept expecting a phone call announcing that the event had been cancelled. None came. About a dozen women showed up, so we proceeded. We agreed that the schedule would be abbreviated and the ladies would be dismissed early.

In the course of the presentations, Mary fidgeted constantly, prompting me to ask her, "Is there something the matter?"

She frowned and shook her head, 'I don't know. I just can't sit still."

Then she revealed how it was her birthday and that her husband, Manny, had surprised her with a beautiful new car. He then insisted that she not cancel the recollection day event but drive to Malibu from their home in Escondido, some 150 miles distant. He had secretly conspired with their grown sons and daughter to surprise her with a birthday dinner party at a local restaurant that evening. At the same time he was eager to inspect the site of their planned new home, designed by their architect son, on a Malibu bluff.

As we concluded the day's conferences, Mary presented each lady with a greeting card of my design, featuring a yellow rose bearing the message: "Thorns Have Roses." "It's always been my favorite," she declared to everyone.

At 7:00 that evening an urgent call came. "Come down right away to my home in the Malibu colony."

"Is there something wrong?" I asked, suddenly alarmed.

"Manny was killed," the caller said.

On arriving, I learned the grim details. Manny had lost his footing on the land's edge and tumbled to the rocks below, severing his spinal cord. Rescuers fought valiantly to shield him from the raging waves pounding the shore. They dared not move him for fear of aggravating his injuries. Paramedics finally brought his bleeding, lifeless body up from the rocks.

Mary was in the home of a caring neighbor, surrounded by grieving friends. When I entered she came into my arms, sobbing and broken, in a state of shock.

"Was your agitation this morning a premonition that some dreadful thing was going to happen?" I asked in a whisper.

All she could say was, "I can't even talk about it. People would think I'm crazy…"

At the sunset of life...
"I will come back to take you with me,
so that where I am
you may be too."

(Jn 14:3)

Close Parentheses

"Caskets Have No Business Being So Small..." read the headline quoting a person attending a funeral. But this was no ordinary funeral. They were burying a four-year-old girl, still an innocent baby. She was one of two young victims run down and killed by a car. But this was not an accident. The grisly fact was that the driver intentionally plowed his car into a pre-school yard full of playing children.

How could someone commit such an unthinkable act? It was later revealed that the driver had been rejected by his lover. Enraged, his sick way to get even was to find and destroy innocent victims. When he drove past the schoolyard he actually turned back and deliberately aimed his car at the playing children.

Images of horrified, grief-stricken and disbelieving parents, teachers and schoolchildren filled the pages of newspapers and TV screens. Death had once more reaped all too-young, innocent lives.

Most people couldn't help but ask why this carefree little girl who was so beautiful and filled with so much love and promise had to die. In the aftermath, people vented their fury, frustration and hatred toward the insane driver. "It's not fair!" many raged. "Make him pay with his own life."

Fair? Are life and death matters of fairness? Is it fair that I am alive? Do I have a right to be alive and, once alive, to live a long, trouble-free life?

It's quite humbling and unnerving to have to admit honestly that I don't. At this happy moment, I am breathing, feeling, thinking, conscious, aware—all without really having much to do with it. I sustain my life with a modicum of effort: eat, sleep, and move. It's easy and automatic. But then some day it will stop—or be stopped, whether suddenly and violently by a tragic accident or a criminal act, or slowly and painfully by a dreadful disease. Or less dramatically and very naturally, my weary heart will simply fail, exhausted.

In no way am I ever entitled to say that it is unfair when life ends, whatever the circumstances. I should never allow myself to forget that life is at all times a gift. Whether long or short, I ought to cherish it. When I stay aware that life will end sooner than I know, I should prize the blessings of each day and live it as fully and productively as I can. I should never squander it.

As a witty Irish friend put it: "When I wake up in the mornin' I look to me right and look to me left. If I don't see wood, I know I'm still kickin' and all's well."

Depending on whose life it is, it's interesting to consider the vast range of attitudes there are about how long life should be. Think of a lonely, disabled widow whose isolation is intolerable and who would just as soon be dead to be with her beloved; a hated despot whose early assassination would be none too soon; an Alzheimer's patient whose violent, irrational behavior torments the loved ones he no longer recognizes; a condemned criminal awaiting his execution date on death row…

While there are those whose pain and suffering are so severe as to wish they were dead, I think most people would still prefer life, however miserable, over death. Being alive under the direst circumstances is like clutching a log hurtling downstream. I cling to life tenaciously, hoping and grasping at everything possible to prolong it.

"A bird in hand is worth two in a bush" makes good sense. I want to hang onto what I have right now. Tomorrow can take care of tomorrow. Better to be than not to be, even in a world of crime, corruption and disease. Think of the pathetic situation of a patient harnessed to a battery of machines to perform the functions of vital organs indefinitely. How futile is the denial of the reality and inevitability of dying.

Death was a "sister" to St. Francis of Assisi who welcomed her with open arms. She was a friend who arrived in time to put him to rest and to escort him into the kingdom. Francis had been convinced by St. Paul's prediction that "we are not going to die; rather, we shall all be changed—in the twinkling of an eye—and the dead will be raised, imperishable, and our mortal nature will put on immortality. Death is swallowed up in victory. Death, where is your victory? Where is your sting?" Paul taunts triumphantly. (1 Cor 15:51-55)

Just before going to his own death, Jesus consoled his friends, "Don't let your hearts be troubled. Trust in God and trust in me. Believe this, I am going to my Father's house to prepare a place for you. Then I will come back to take you with me, so that where I am, you may be too." (Jn 14:1-6)

A nun once told me, "In my 35 years as a hospital nurse, I have never seen a patient die terrified." And the many documented stories of persons who passed "to the other side" in clinical death when vital signs ceased temporarily, who then experienced awesome, even thrilling encounters with gentle beings and soothing lights, appear to confirm all that the scriptures foretell about life after death.

The most encouraging aspect shared commonly by near-death survivors is their genuine disappointment at having to return to life on this earth. Their foretaste of the beauty and joy to follow is truly what "no eye has ever seen, ears have never heard, and no human mind has ever conceived, all that God has prepared for those who love him." (1 Cor 2:9)

So, why am I so reluctant and afraid ?

P.S. There will be a wedding reception and banquet awaiting all who pass from this life. And guess who will be the host serving at table? None other than the Bridegroom himself, the beloved Jesus who has made it all possible and whose love will never end. His promises and commitment of the New Covenant are unbreakable and everlasting. R.S.V.P.